D1711726

Dedicated in eternal gratitude

to

Ma and Dad

Preface

For the better part of my adult life it has been my personal goal to set down in writing the events of our family in the difficult years we have come to recall as "The Great Depression." We were probably not much different in our experience from millions of other families throughout our great land. So, this story could really be the story of any of those families as well.

As a very young adult, when I first conceived this project, I lacked the necessary skills. All I possessed were memories. But, I kept honing those memories to keep them alive, knowing that some day my dream would become a reality. I learned to type and I learned to write. All the time I kept the dream alive.

I nurtured a family of seven children to adulthood, working full time for 15 of those years.

I took courses at the University of Minnesota and I wrote magazine articles, book and play reviews and news stories for publication. I edited an employee newsletter for Hennepin County Municipal Court.

But most important was the support I received from friends and family. I gained invaluable assistance from my children whose career preparation endowed them with a variety of communications skills, both written and spoken. They read, edited, proofed and criticized my work with familial loyalty and professional know-how.

I received encouragement from a dear friend who has published several books of poetry. The harsh constructive criticism I received from a fine University of Minnesota English professor got me started in the right literary direction.

So, it seems that after all the years of preparation, the time has come for the publication of *The Hungry Years.*

All the incidents herein recorded actually happened. I have made a diligent effort to be accurate. I have researched all events and can certify that they are true. However, the conversations which have been reconstructed to enhance the narrative, are written as they may have occurred. Many of the principals are now deceased or their whereabouts is unknown. Any inaccuracies are unintentional and without malice.

Without the many documents, newspaper clippings, photos and letters that my dear mother saved over the years, this book would not have been possible. Further, I owe a debt of gratitude to my brother, C. Thomas May, known as Cleo in this writing, for his willingness to share his letters to and from the family while he was in CCC Camp. Finally, my husband Calvin has been a patient prince through it all.

Rowena May Pope

Designed by my dear friend, Sylvia Carsen

CONTENTS

Chapter One

Fine at the Start

"Judge Weds Pair Clad In Overalls," quipped the headline of the August 11, 1920 evening edition of the *Kirksville Daily Express*. The couple to whom the headline referred was Thomas May and Lulah Sevits. In retrospect, the facetious headline implying that they were improperly attired, seemed to portend the difficult years that lay ahead for them.

Tom and Lulah met when he accompanied his sister Cassie and twin sister Sylvia from their home in Putnam County to revival meetings at Hazel Creek Church. The girls developed a great friendship with Lulah and her twin sister Beulah. Thomas made no secret of the fact that he wanted to get to know Lulah better.

About a year later, after Sylvia had married and was expecting her first child, she and her husband Peter asked Lulah to come and stay as their hired girl for Sylvia's convalescent period. Because Tom spent so much time with Pete and Sylvia, he would, at last, have his opportunity to get better acquainted with Lulah.

They saw each other just about every day during the two weeks Lulah worked for Pete and Sylvia. And after a brief courtship, they fell in love and began to plan for their wedding day. The appointed day had seemed like eons away.

They came on that August 10 morning the 15 miles from Lulah's home in north central Adair County, by buckboard driven by her younger brothers, Forest and Harve, from the farm to the train depot in Sublette, and by train to Kirksville. A Model T Ford taxicab took them from the depot to Sylvia's home on Mill Street. When the driver stopped, Thomas jumped out, paid the ten-cent fare and helped Lulah out of the car with her traveling bag.

Sylvia, bubbling with excitement, ran to meet them at the gate. She threw her arms around each one and hugged them soundly.

"Oh," she exclaimed, "I couldn't have waited another minute! I'm so glad you made it O.K."

"Now, Tom," she directed, "put Lulah's bag in the spare bed-room, while I pour you both a cup of coffee. I got up early this morning and made your favorite rolls. I know you will both have one, won't you?"

After the three had chatted for a while at the kitchen table, Tom asked to be excused and set out on foot to the courthouse to apply for the marriage license. While he was downtown, he talked to Judge Pickell to arrange for their wedding vows to be exchanged in his presence on the following morning, Wednesday, August 11.

Lulah asked, "How is my little Katheryn?"

Sylvia responded, "Come and see."

"Oh," gasped Lulah, "how she has grown! And she is so beautiful. Do you have anyone to take care of her tomorrow while we go see the judge?"

"Oh, yes," Sylvia assured, "I have a good neighbor who will be glad to take care of her while we are gone."

When Peter came home from the coal mine and after he had taken his bath, they all shared a fine dinner together. Peter's English wasn't very good. He had just been in America for a couple of years. He was a long way from Turin, Italy, but he was happy with his new family and happy, too, to have a good job in the mine.

At about nine the next morning the little taxi chugged its way up to the front of the house. It caught no one by surprise with its resound-ing "oogah." They were ready.

Thomas was impeccable in his dark blue suit, clean-shaven and his dark hair combed back. Lulah was radiant in her blue silk plaid taffeta blouse paired with a fully flared dark blue silk skirt. She had meticulously ratted her dark brown hair into a bouffant Gibson Girl style adorned with a matching ribbon. Sylvia, dressed in her best attire, accompanied them to be their witness.

The taxi stopped in front of Judge Pickell's office. Thomas, dis-playing his best manners, helped his sister and his bride-to-be out of the car. As the trio approached, they could see that the shades were drawn. It was obvious no one was there. Thomas didn't panic, however. Instead, he telephoned the judge at his home, from the drugstore next door. The judge apologized for having forgotten their appointment and explained that he had closed the office so that he could get some work done around the house. He closed their conversation by saying, "Come on over to the house and we'll tie the knot."

Thomas nervously removed the neatly folded white linen handkerchief from his back pocket and wiped the sweat from his forehead.

"The judge said he was sorry about the mix up, but he said we could come over to his house. That's all right with you, ain't it, Lulah?"

Relieved that their plans had not been spoiled, Lulah replied, "Of course, it's all right."

Once again Thomas summoned the taxi, and once again they were on their way.

As they pulled up in front of the two-story, white frame house, Judge Pickell, perched about half way up on a ladder leaning against the shady side of the house, wearing white overalls, dipped his brush into the paint bucket. As he stroked the brush along the surface of the wood, he became aware of the presence of his guests and called out, "I'll be right down!"

As he reached the bottom rung of the ladder, the judge picked up a turpentine-saturated rag and wiped the paint from his hands. He extended his right hand in a gesture of friendship and welcome to Thomas, saying, "Would you mind terribly if I didn't change clothes? I want to get this painting done before it rains."

Tom looked to Lulah for a nod of approval. "We don't mind," he replied, "overalls are fine."

After inviting them into the house, in the presence of his 14-year-old daughter Marian and Tom's sister Sylvia, Judge Pickell, wearing paint splotched overalls, pronounced the couple husband and wife.

Tom and Lulah's heritage bore a striking resemblance. Each of them had a twin sister; they both came from large pioneer families whose measure of worth was hard work; and because they were children of the soil, they were prepared for only one vocation—farming. Their goal was to work as hired help for other farmers until they could save up enough money to buy a place of their own.

They could not have chosen a more inopportune time in history to achieve their goal. Although historians have labeled the period of time from the crash of the stock market in October, 1929, until the entry of America into World War II, as the Great Depression, farmers experienced an economic pinch even earlier. Isolationist policy of the administrations following World War I and high tariffs under the Fordney-McCumber Act had left farmers with huge crop

The Sevits Twins with handsome brother Dewey

surpluses and plummeting farm prices. Foreign trade had come to a standstill. Banks failed, factories ceased production, stores closed, local governments were unable to collect taxes and mortgage foreclosure was forced upon many land owners.

And just when it appeared that President Roosevelt's New Deal farm programs would save the farmer, the nation suffered widespread droughts in 1934 and again in 1936, making it impossible for farmers to reap an appreciable harvest.

A third of the people in our nation were directly involved in the struggle for survival in that period. Because an even greater number of young persons today share the heritage of this unique time in history, and yet have little or no firsthand information concerning the way families lived, it is for them I have chosen to recall the experiences of our family during those difficult years.

Thomas and Lulah May, known affectionately to us, their children, as "Dad" and "Ma," were prepared for hard work and sacrifices, but they could not have imagined the hardships they would be called upon to endure as they entered the joy of that August day back in 1920.

In the early years of their marriage, Dad and Ma had no difficulty finding good employers who provided reasonable wages and comfortable housing. If they moved from one employer to another, it was by choice. A bigger house to provide room for their growing brood of children, a school closer to their home or better wages were incentives that would entice them to move. However, as conditions worsened for the agricultural community, opportunities for farm laborers lessened.

Missouri farms, unless they stretched along the river bottoms, required much effort to reap a reasonable yield of produce. Because the soil was poor and the hilly terrain caused rapid run-off of rainfall, Missouri farmers made less profit per acre of land, even in good times, than farmers in Iowa, for instance.

By the time the country was well into the Great Depression of the 1930s, Dad was experiencing extreme difficulty finding a land owner who produced enough to afford to hire any help. Because the fiscal farm year ran from March 1 to March 1, Dad was assured of a job and a place for his family to live for at least a year if he could just find a farmer who would sign him on. Some years a farmer who felt he could afford help discovered that he was harnessed to a financial burden, usually before the year's end. He would have no choice but to give notice to his hired help.

For Dad this meant sleepless nights and long discouraging searches for another job. For Ma it presented the upsetting consequence of preparing her children for another move in the midst of the school year.

Some years with no contract at all, Dad rented a house, normally provided for hired help, and worked by the day for anyone who would give him a day's work. The going rate of pay fell somewhere between 75 cents and $1 a day, and if under contract, a house, a garden spot and a cow to milk. By any economic standards, this kind of income stretched to the limit would scarcely provide bare necessities.

By some stroke of genius Ma and Dad instilled in my six brothers, my sister and me a sense of dignity and a feeling of self-worth. We

*Beulah with baby Clifford and Ma holding
the little sailor, Cleo*

Dad, Ma and the boys in better times

*Barefoot boys perched on a patient pony with
Dad's steadying hand*

had little of the world's goods, but because we were surrounded by nature and the wonder of the universe, we were somehow oblivious to our poverty. We knew the whip-poor-will's call and could describe a hummingbird in detail. Dad taught us to respect song birds' nests and to pick wild flowers carefully, leaving the roots undisturbed. Ma taught us to "tell the truth and shun the devil."

They respected learning as a valuable tool, and although Ma's formal education was limited to the eighth grade and Dad's to the ninth, they were vitally interested in history, politics and current events. Remarkably, they always provided the daily newspaper which they considered to be as essential as food or clothing. Our library consisted of two books—the Holy Bible and the "doctor book." But we read anything we could get our hands on borrowed from neighbors and relatives and from the limited country school libraries.

Because Ma and Dad were from differing political backgrounds, they often engaged in animated, sometimes heated, discussions concerning the effectiveness of President Roosevelt's programs. Even though they had been known to walk to the polls and cast opposite votes, they considered anyone derelict who did not exercise his right to vote.

They believed that a person's integrity was his most valuable possession. Whatever they taught us, they demonstrated in the lives they lived publicly and privately, not only by precept, but by example as well. Reluctant to despair, ever willing to sacrifice for the good of their children, Dad and Ma brought our family through insurmountable hardships to survive the Great Depression.

Chapter Two

By the Sweat of His Brow

Farm labor, Dad's chosen vocation, was the oldest and the most back-breaking work known to man, perhaps because man walks upright and the soil is beneath his feet.

Work began in the early spring when Dad and the boys, as each grew old enough to help, gathered up the debris from the fields and stacked it in giant piles. When the wind was calm and they had taken care to prevent the spread of fire, they lit the huge bonfire. Tall black columns of smoke rose skyward. The aroma of burning corn stalks signaled the approaching vernal equinox. After all the trash was consumed by fire and March winds had evaporated the moisture from winter snows and early spring rains, plowing time arrived.

Because few farms were mechanized, plowing was a one-man, two-horse job. Although a limited number of farmers owned gang plows or sulkies, the walking plow was the primary tool for breaking the soil. Simply constructed, it was made of three main parts. The iron beam, literally the backbone of the plow, provided an opening at one end to attach the harness so the horses could pull it. At the opposite end sturdy wooden handles, mounted about waist high, made it possible for the plowman to guide the plow for straight furrows. At the bottom were the working parts. The plowshare, sharp, made of steel and designed to cut deep into the earth, was aided by the moldboard and the landside which turned the earth and facilitated easy manipulation of the plow.

Dad loved the smell of freshly turned earth. His love for the soil made him a perfectionist in every phase of tending it. He prided himself in his ability to plow straight, clean furrows at the rate of an acre or more per day.

Beginning as early as possible in the morning, usually shortly after sunrise, Dad started his long day plowing. He worked closely with the horses calling out "Gee" and "Haw" as necessary to keep them moving in the right direction. The harness line was a continuous leather strap which looped around his waist at the lowest point and across his shoulder at the highest. Attached to the bit in each horse's mouth, the slightest pressure on the strap indicated to the horse his master's wishes.

It is not quite clear whether the horses really understood "Gee" and "Haw" because they were always used with the pressure on the harness lines. Perhaps saying the words aloud gave the plowman occasion to break the silence without appearing ridiculous.

Another common command or perhaps encouragement would be a better term, was a sound made by clicking the tongue against the side of one's cheek. Dad always seemed to be carrying on a conversation with the horses as he urged, "Come on, Ribbon." "Now, straighten up there, Dan." "A couple more turns around the field and we'll stop for a rest."

All day long the wearying process continued, day after day, with stops for both man and beast to have a cool drink of water and a short rest at lunch time.

By mid- or late-April the plowing was completed. Dad loaded the plow on the wagon and returned it to the machine shed for cleaning and oiling for storage until the next spring.

His work far from finished, plowing was only the first step in preparation of the soil. To facilitate planting, the soil must be reduced to a finer consistency. Two methods for achieving this were employed. First, Dad mounted a horse-drawn machine equipped with a series of sharp disks 12 to 18 inches in diameter fixed on an axle through the center and drove it across the field to slice the large chunks of soil into smaller pieces. Finally, the harrow, a machine like a giant garden rake, broke the soil into finer particles and smoothed the surface. The harrow differed from the disk because it provided no seat for the operator.

In every step of soil preparation there was a race against time. If the disking or harrowing was interrupted by rain, of course, when the fields dried the process would necessarily be repeated.

Seed corn, carefully selected in the fall harvest and preserved through the winter season, was now brought forth for planting.

The corn planter held about a half bushel of seed corn in each of the two containers located on the driver's right and left. A rotary motion caused by the movement of the planter, emitted grains of corn at regular intervals in holes dug by little shovel-like blades located directly below each of the seed containers. Dad kept the horses moving at a steady gait to provide for consistent emission of corn seeds.

In Missouri, corn planting should be completed by the early part of May. After about two weeks of germination, the corn plants appear along with the weeds. Most farmers owned cultivators, which with their series of hoe-like shovels attached to a frame that could be raised or lowered by the operator, were capable of clearing weeds at a faster rate than manually operated hoes. However, to attack the weeds with a concerted effort, men ran the cultivators and boys hoed, at the rate of 35 cents per day for boys and 75 cents to $1 for men.

Hoeing corn is a tedious, back-bending and seemingly never ending chore. Because the weeds are much more prolific and hardier than corn plants, the hoeing process had to be repeated at least three times before the corn could be "laid by."

In the summer of 1934, when we lived at the Sandry place, Cleo, 13, and Clifford, 11, were working in the field with Dad, hoeing corn while Dad rode the cultivator. To hoe corn one must be slightly bent over, constantly on the lookout for weeds, continuously chopping and loosening the soil. After hoeing corn for seven hours with only a short break for dinner and an occasional stop for a drink of water, Dad and the boys began to long for evening and supper time. Their blue chambray shirts bore etchings of dried salt from the perspiration freely given off by their tired bodies exposed to the sun's hot rays. A big red or blue bandana, wet from wiping sweat, dangled from the hip pocket of each pair of faded blue denim overalls.

When Dad came in from the field and the sun was still high in the hot summer afternoon sky, Ma knew something was wrong. Because neither Clifford nor Cleo had come in with him, she feared the worst for their sake. Before Ma could ask questions, Dad began to speak:

"Lulah, I'm sorry, but I had to do it. I warned Bill the last time he hit Howard with his cane that I would stop him if he ever did it again. Well, this afternoon he began thrashing the boy and I knocked him down."

Howard, about 16 at the time of the incident, was an orphan the old man had taken in to raise.

Dad continued, "He said he was going to go into town to have me arrested. I'm sure the sheriff will be here to take me to jail before nightfall. Cleo and Cliff saw it happen, so they know what to expect, but I don't know what to tell the young'ns."

Ma stood there, mouth agape, half hearing what Dad was saying, not wanting to believe what she was hearing. Then prepared for the worst, she simply responded, "Don't worry, Tom, we'll manage somehow."

As Dad had predicted, the sheriff did come with a warrant for his arrest. He was taken to Kirksville, the county seat, some 12 or 15 miles away. When he had not returned in two or three days as Ma had hoped, and because she had no way to communicate with him, Ma made up her mind to get someone to take her into town to see what would ultimately happen to Dad and to us.

Mr. Sandry owed Dad wages, but there was neither food nor money in the house. Ma was pregnant and not feeling too well, besides. But she organized a plan of action. She sent Cleo and Cliff to Novinger on foot about four or five miles with a note to her brother Harvey asking him to come to take her into town to see what was going to happen to Tom.

Because she had never left us alone before, Ma spent some time preparing us for her absence.

"Cleo, you will be in charge."

"The rest of you, do as he says."

"Rene," her nickname for me, "you are to take care of baby Shirley."

"Cliff, you help Cleo with the meals and dishes."

"Jimmy and Milton, you are not to be scrapping. Keep out of mischief and look after little Robert."

Then a final admonition to Cliff and Cleo, "Be careful with the fire."

Harvey arrived early the next morning, and after repeating the orders once more, Ma got in the car with him and they drove away.

The hours droned on endlessly until her return in the evening. She praised us for carrying out her instructions and heaved a sigh of relief that we were all safe and sound.

Ma hadn't gone begging for Dad's release—that was below her dignity, and Dad's. Instead, she had simply told the sheriff of our plight. We had no food nor money. He was sympathetic and offered to do what he could. He bent the rules a little and allowed her to visit with Dad for a few minutes.

Just at dusk a big car rolled down the narrow lane to our house in the woods. A man armed with a pistol strapped to his belt and a shiny badge pinned to his shirt ambled up the path as we peered from the windows. He was carrying a big box of groceries, obviously for us. He didn't have to knock; Ma met him at the door.

"Mrs. May," he said, "we can't do anything about getting Tom released until in the morning when the judge can hear the matter, but we did do something about the food. Maybe these things will tide you over until Tom can get back to work."

Reluctantly, Ma thanked the deputy sheriff. She knew we needed the food, but handouts were humiliating.

She swallowed her pride and proceeded to check out the contents of the box. Our eyes bulged with wonder as she took out, one by one, bananas, oranges, Jello, cheese, lunch meat, "baker's bread" and other ready-edible perishable food items. Ma could have shown more appreciation for beans, corn meal, flour, lard, sugar and coffee. She knew this box of impractical goodies would be consumed in a day or two.

I was only five years old, but on Sunday morning when Mr. Sandry, the Sunday School superintendent, stood before the congregation to pray, the black eye Dad had given him for thrashing Howard, reminded me of the humiliation Dad suffered from being jailed, and I was bitter. Somehow, I could not equate the love he proclaimed with the revenge he practiced.

Dad came home the next day, but we never talked about the incident. As for Mr. Sandry, he brought Dad's back wages along with our notice to move in the spring, but for now he expected business to continue as usual.

As soon as the corn was "laid by," it was haying time. In plowing and planting it was important to get into the fields early. But haymaking imposed a measure of patience on the hay makers. Because of the heavy dewfall in the summer nights, cutting was delayed until seven or eight in the morning to allow the sun to thoroughly dry the grass. To compensate for the later start, the men worked later in the evening.

The hay-mowing machine, equipped with a sickle about six feet in length and lowered to within four or five inches of the surface of the earth, was pulled at a steady speed by a team of horses while the clipping action on the sickle bar cut the tall grass down. After the grass was cut, a horse drawn sulky rake followed close behind the sickle, raking the hay into windrows for drying.

Dad's favorite job in the hay was stacking. After the freshly cut hay had been allowed to dry, usually for one full day, one of the boys drove the hay wagon while the men walked along pitching the hay up onto the wagon. When it was fully loaded, the driver took the wagon to a predetermined location for the hay to be stacked.

Stacking required a certain measure of skill. Because the stacks had to withstand the wind and rain, the stacker took great care to distribute the hay compactly and evenly, as the men pitched the hay to him. Because there were so many procedures to be performed simultaneously, farmers usually arranged to work together to harvest their hay. In addition to the stacks left out in the fields, they filled the hay mows in their barns to capacity.

In the summer of 1936 when we lived at the Albert Sullivan place, Dad and 15-year-old Cleo had a haying job about ten to 12 miles from our home. At the rate of five miles per hour, walking took them at least two hours to reach their destination. This meant starting a hard day's work in the hayfield with two hours' energy already used up. They worked hard, Dad stacking and Cleo driving the hay wagon. Dad had admonished Cleo when he got the job for him, "This is a man's job; you'll have to work like a man."

They looked forward to the reward of a big noon meal and a much deserved rest. When they came up to the house for dinner, the housewife called to Cleo, "Come here, boy."

Cleo obediently responded.

"Now, take this pail and go down to the pond and get water for the chickens," she commanded.

Dad was on his feet in seconds and up to the house in less than a minute.

"Oh, no you don't," he warned. "This boy has been working all morning the same as everyone else. You have no right to ask him to carry water on his lunch hour."

Then he put his arm around Cleo and said, "Come on son; rest a while before dinner."

When the day in the hay field ended, Dad and Cleo started their trek homeward, arriving after dark. There was no time for amenities. After a quick bite to eat they dropped into bed for a much too short night's rest.

Small grain harvesting usually followed the haying time and it, too, involved a great number of operations at the same time. For that reason, threshing wheat and oats dictated a cooperative effort. The owner of the threshing machine went from farm to farm during the small grain harvest time. Farmers were expected to provide the necessary manpower.

The threshing machine, an exciting wonder for everyone to behold, belched smoke skyward and spewed the grain into the wagon. The straw landed in a huge pile behind the thresher.

In addition to the work Dad did, plowing, planting and harvesting for others, he plowed, planted and supervised the cultivating and harvesting of our own garden. Even though tending a vegetable

Threshing machine belching smoke and many hands stacking straw

garden is hard work, Dad found joy and satisfaction in watching the plants grow into maturity and yield their bountiful produce. He planned his garden with the precision of an engineer. He prepared the soil carefully and lovingly. He designed the furrows to allow for proper drainage. To make certain the rows would be straight and uniform, he sighted the first row against some fixed object and then with stakes and binder twine measured the succeeding rows. Weeds were not permitted. Rabbits and insects presented a more difficult problem. Armed with a tin can filled about one fourth full of kerosene, the boys and I hand picked potato bugs and exterminated them in the kerosene. Dad always praised us depending upon the number of bugs we had caught. The boys trapped rabbits with self-improvised snares, a wire noose with a bit of corn tied to dangle in front of the opening so that when the rabbit put its head through to grab the corn, the noose would tighten around its neck. In addition to protecting the garden, the rabbits the boys caught provided meat for our table.

Dad always put in his garden at the earliest possible time because we depended so heavily on the produce for meals. He grew Golden Bantam and Shoepeg sweet corn, Kentucky Wonder pole beans, cobbler potatoes, Rutger and Earliana tomatoes, Early Alaska peas, Flat Dutch cabbage, Black Seeded Simpson lettuce, Icicle and French Breakfast radishes, Long Green pickling cucumbers, Stringless Greenpod green beans, Sweet Spanish and Bermuda onions, and a host of other commonly used vegetables.

Early autumn brought corn harvest time. Cutting and shocking corn, done manually were slow, back-breaking procedures. Cutting the stalks required a long sharp knife; carrying them to a central shock required a strong back.

Dad's corn knife, honed razor sharp by regular whetting on his pocket whetstone, consisted of a blade about two and a half feet long by three inches wide and a hardwood handle shaped for easy gripping. Dad had a reputation for being able to cut and shock corn faster and more neatly than nearly anyone around. Cutting and shocking corn were lonely chores. A shock contained the stalks cut from 144 hills of corn or 12 hills by 12 rows. Dad chopped the stalks, one by one, and when he had collected an armful, he stacked them together, wigwam fashion, and tied them with heavy binder twine. Later when the mature corn had had time to dry, the ears were picked from the stalks and loaded onto the wagon and brought in to the corn crib for winter storage. The stalks were fed to the livestock.

When the harvest season was over, Dad mended fences and cut fence posts and firewood. The boys usually went with him to the woods. Dad felled the trees with his sharp, double-bladed axe and then the boys took turns manning the other end of a crosscut saw to cut the logs into necessary lengths. To split the tough oak logs, Dad drove wedges in with a sledge hammer and then finished the splitting operation with the axe.

Because little farm work was available during the winter months, Dad developed other sources of income. He traveled great distances on foot along creeks and branches seeking out the dens and runs of fur-bearing animals. He prepared boards suitable for stretching pelts and repaired his spring steel traps. The traps had two powerful jaws with a trigger where bait was placed. When the animal attempted to get the bait, the trap jaws were sprung and the animal could not get free. Dad ran his traps every day, the 20-mile round trip taking him into late afternoon. When he got home the skinning and pelt dressing process took place by lamp light. Mink pelts were the most valuable, followed by muskrat, raccoon, weasel, skunk and opossum. Red fox pelts, also quite valuable were a rare catch for Dad.

Sometimes Ma wrapped one of the soft mink pelts around her neck and Dad would say, "Some day I'll have a fur coat made for you out of mink pelts I've caught myself."

Ma responded quite seriously, "How many pelts do you think it would take to make a full-length, double-breasted, princess-styled coat?" She didn't really expect an answer, and as she slowly withdrew the mink pelt from around her shoulders, stroking the soft fur one last time and handing it back to Dad, "Maybe next year," she would conclude wistfully.

Setting the traps, running the lines and dressing the pelts were just the preparatory steps. Dad earned no money until the pelts were sold. Sometimes he walked to the nearest general store to market his furs. A fur buyer came to the store about once a week. If Dad had more pelts than he could carry, he took only his best sample of each variety and arranged for the buyer to come to the house to examine the balance. What an exciting day it was when we heard the fur buyer's old pickup truck rattling up in front of the house! He offered Dad a pipeful of good tobacco, and usually he had a stick of chewing gum or a piece of candy for each of us kids. Then he and Dad got

Dad displaying prime pelts

down to the serious business of fur trading. After the long discussion of the assets and liabilites of the goods being sold, Dad always had money in his hands when the buyer left. Now Dad could walk to the store to get coffee, sugar, lard, flour, tobacco, and maybe a dime's worth of corn candy or gum drops.

When Dad sold his furs, Ma got out the Sears and Roebuck mail-order catalog. Now she could order the flannelette she had been needing to make the baby some gowns. And if it were my turn, I got to order new shoes. Dad turned to the page with the foot measuring chart on it. After following the instructions to the letter, he added a full size, making certain the shoes would not be outgrown before they were worn out. He always selected only the sturdiest, most practical styles. I can recall looking longingly on the black patent leather Mary Janes and fantasizing how I would whirl around in my white ruffled organdy dress, Mary Janes and white anklets. The dream quickly vanished as Dad patiently explained why I was getting the high-topped, brown leather shoes: "These will last a long time and besides, they have good leather uppers that I can half-sole."

When Ma had carefully completed the order blank, we watched for the mail carrier to come. We knew he would stop at our box to leave the daily paper, so we were certain not to miss him.

When he stopped we bought a money order to cover the cost of the items ordered and a three-cent stamp for the envelope. We hurried back to the house with the mail and the change and marked the calendar so we could count the days until delivery.

The reason Dad bought only shoes with sturdy leather uppers was that he did all our shoe repairing. He had interchangeable shoe lasts, made of cast iron in small, medium and large to accommodate all our shoes. He mounted the proper last on his matching iron staff. He cut soles from a sheet of heavy leather just large enough to cover the bottom of the shoe. With his awl and tackhammer, he drove the small-headed nails deep into the leather, clenching the ends against the surface of the metal last. Sometimes, if a tack wasn't clenched completely smooth, one might have a sore foot and a blood-stained sock after walking to school or church.

Dad repaired our rubber overshoes with a tire repair kit. We were embarrassed with our green and red patches, but we never had leaky overshoes.

Because Dad was extremely nearsighted he didn't hunt with a gun. But he was an expert gunsmith and had been known to take a seemingly irreparable gun and restore it to usefulness. He also had a knack for repairing clocks.

Dad's avocation was a source of irritation for Ma. He loved to play poker. When he was completely out of work, Dad would organize a poker game and be gone all night long. He used to say the only way to win at poker is to run the game. I don't recall his ever losing. One morning he came home with goodies for everyone and $24 dollars in cash besides. It was more money than Ma had seen in a long time. Her facade of anger soon cracked into smiles as she joined into the joy and excitement of the treats he had brought.

Sometimes his winnings were not quite as negotiable. Occasionally he brought home a jacket or a blanket or a pair of rubber boots. Once, to Ma's total dismay, he brought home a 'coon hound. Dad assured her that the hound was valuable and that all he needed to do was to find a buyer. After the dog chewed up some clothes on the clothesline, Ma put her foot down and demanded the dog's removal.

By the winter of 1937-38 Dad knew that he could no longer depend on farm work for a living. There had to be something better, somewhere. He and one of his brothers and a nephew who owned a beat-up old Buick, drove to Waterloo, Iowa, an industrial city, looking for work.

That trip ended in near-tragedy and with no job. Here is Dad's own description of the events in a letter written to Cleo on November 4, 1937, at the CCC Camp in Troy, Missouri.

"Dear Son,

Will write you a few lines to let you know I am feeling very well. I have been so sore I could hardly walk for 2 weeks, but I guess I am lucky to be alive. I will tell you how it happened: Pood May was driving a big Buick. There was Sol, Scott Pointer, Cap Tarr, his Wife and baby, Dale Gregory, Pood and myself in the car. Pood was driving about 65 miles per hour. He drove around a car, got straightened out again. There was another car about 150 feet ahead of him—lots of traffic—cars on both sides of the highway and the car in front. Pood's car was going 65 miles per hour and the car in front put on his brakes to stop without any signal. Pood's car didn't have any brakes, but the emergency brake, and you see they only stop the rear wheels. The man in front had four-wheel brakes and stopped so quick. Pood tried to go around him, but a big car pulled up just as he started to go around him. He either had to hit the car that stopped or take to the ditch. He took to the ditch. Now all this happened in less than 10 seconds. So you can see his brakes were no good to him. We rolled over 2 or 3 times, and believe me I thought we would all get killed. The first time we went over, something hit me across the chest and knocked me silly for about 15 minutes. Pood got his fingers cut to the bone in several places. Sol had his head cut open on top; they had to take several stitches. Cap Tarr got cut pretty bad; so did Scott Pointer. Dale Gregory, Cap's wife and baby didn't get hurt much. How anyone got out alive is a miracle. The car was torn all to hell. There wasn't a piece of glass as big as a dollar after the wreck.

Well, I will close. I thought you would want to know how it happened. I think I will get all right although I am feeling pretty tough yet. I would have written sooner, but I supposed Lulah had told you all about it. Take care of yourself and be a good boy.

Your father, Thomas

P.S. Sol got a half gallon jar of jelly mashed all over his head. He sure looked funny!"

Dad's amazing sense of humor prevailed over the despair he must have felt when the job he had hoped to get was given to another.

He had reached the point of total despair when Dad learned that Adair County would be participating in President Roosevelt's Works Progress Administration. Commonly called WPA, it was a federal program designed to undertake public works projects for municipalities such as street, parks and sewer and water improvements in cases where the local governments could not provide the funds.

Dad wasted no time in making application for a job. Since he qualified by having enough dependents, he was hired at $1.50 per day. His new job took him to a rock quarry on the other side of the county. It was no surprise that we would have to move. This time our move took us to Sublette, a tiny hamlet with a general store and a filling station. We were on the main highway and the railroad ran through the town. It was a new way of life for us. Cars and trains sped by night and day.

People made jokes about the WPA, but Dad always said the hardest work he ever did was smashing large rocks into small ones with a sledge hammer.

This work could not have been the most rewarding and occasionally on payday the men kicked up their heels a bit.

One such payday evening it was dark and Dad was not home yet. Ma, rolling out pie dough by lamplight on the kitchen table, stopped when she heard a car drive up. It was Dad and the other WPA workers he rode back and forth to work with. They were all laughing and talking boisterously. When Dad emerged from the car, it was obvious he was in an altered state. We had never seen anyone intoxicated before and especially not Dad. But there was no other explanation—he was drunk.

Up to the porch steps he staggered, smiling and swaying. At first Ma was relieved he was safe, but her anger soon came to the surface. "Tom, what in the world is the meaning of this?" she questioned, knowing full well she would not get a reasonable answer.

"Now you just listen here, lady," he retorted in garbled tongue, "you sound like a crazed Ethiopian!" With that he staggered to the rocking chair in the next room and plopped down.

Robert and I, totally awe-stricken and a bit terrified, decided to render him harmless. We removed the strings from our shoes and tied his hands to the wooden arms of the rocking chair.

After the initial excitement subsided, Ma had Cliff help her get Dad undressed and into bed. We went to bed, too, but we didn't go to sleep right away. We chattered and giggled well into the night. We never did figure out why Dad called Ma a "crazed Ethiopian." Furthermore, no one ever asked him.

Chapter Three

Lye Soap and
Pine-Splintered Floors

If Dad's work was produced by the sweat of his brow, Ma's work was drawn from the fiber of her soul. The houses we lived in from the time I was four years old until I was about ten presented a challenge in homemaking that only a woman dedicated to survival for her children could meet.

Substandard in every way and often infested with bedbugs and rodents, many of these houses had been moved to their locations from Connelsville, Missouri, a coal mining boom town. The mining company had built a great number of square, four-room houses with pyramid shaped roofs to house their miners. When the coal vein expired, the mining company gave up its mining rights and made arrangements to move the houses from the land. Offered for sale at a low price with the stipulation they be moved at the buyers' expense, the houses gave farmers the opportunity to provide low-cost housing for their hired help. Some who could not afford hired help saw the low-priced houses as a possible investment for rental income. Some of the houses were moved as far as 20 miles. The moving resulted in shattered windows, cracked and broken plaster, warped door frames and bulging floors. At their destination they were set in place on as few concrete blocks as were absolutely necessary for foundation with no further restorative work undertaken.

Other houses we lived in had been the original family home of the present land owners a generation away. Sometimes, one of the sons built a new house for his family and when the old parents passed away, the original family home was designated for the hired help. As the original homestead, these houses usually boasted seven or eight rooms. However, as the years passed and the original occupants died, the houses deteriorated. The common denominator of the four-room mine houses and the seven-room homesteads was that when we lived in them only three rooms were habitable. Ten of us ate, slept and grew in those three rooms, the kitchen, the front room and the bedroom.

Ma's wood-burning cookstove dominated the kitchen. Made of cast iron with a surface of about three feet by four feet, a fire box of about a foot in width and a foot in depth opening at the front and with removable lids on the top, a cleanout for ashes below the fire box, and a large oven to the right of the fire box, the total unit weighed several hundred pounds. The cast-iron wood-burning unit rested on shiny steel legs, a separate section of the stove. Our cook-stove was equipped with a warming oven that rose about two feet above the cooking surface at the rear. We used it primarily for the storage of skillets and pan lids that were used every day. Because of the settling of soot and dust from ashes, long-term storage proved futile. Ma always wished she had a reservoir for keeping water hot, but she consoled herself with the thought that she had enough trouble getting the boys to carry enough water to keep the tea kettle filled.

Close to the stove we kept the washstand equipped with the water bucket and dipper, the wash pan and soap dish. Strategically located between the stove and washstand for the collection of waste stood the embarrassment of every household, the "slop" bucket. Most of the water which was carried in for cooking, washing dishes, canning or laundry must necessarily be carried out as waste.

The long rectangular kitchen table was more than just a place for eating. Unpainted and covered with a tattered oil cloth, it provided the space for food preparation and dishwashing. We children sat on either of two long benches at the front and back sides, while Ma sat at one end on the stool chair with Dad at the other end on the "good" chair, so-called because it was complete with a back and all the rungs in place.

The cupboard, called a "safe," which protected our few dishes, was about 40 inches wide, 16 inches deep and about 5½ feet tall. The double doors at the top and bottom displayed intricate designs effected from holes punched in the tin inserts in the space normally occupied by glass in a china cabinet. Between the two sets of doors were the drawers for storage of flatware.

A big cabinet provided storage space for staple goods. In one of two large bins we kept flour and in the other, sugar, corn meal, beans, rice and oatmeal. The shelves above kept the baking powder, salt, spices and flavorings within easy reach. Below the sheet-

aluminum covered work surface were two large bread boards—one
floured for kneading dough and the other permanently grease
stained from cooling freshly baked loaves of bread.

Just as the wood-burning cookstove provided the source of
energy for the activities in the kitchen, so the huge black coal- and
wood-burning heating stove radiated the warmth around which the
functions in the front room revolved. During the day-time hours fuel
was added at regular intervals to maintain a constant temperature.
At night Dad banked the fire with a specially cut block of wood and
a large chunk of coal, if we had it. Banking, a process insuring slow
burning and yet not allowing the fire to go out, could only be
achieved with a thick, well seasoned block of wood and/or a large,
solid chunk of slow-burning coal. The draft had to be reduced to a
minimum giving a limited supply of oxygen thereby slowing the
burning process. When morning came, Dad got up early, shook the
ashes down, opened the draft damper and added dry wood to get a
quick hot fire. With the fire shovel he took some of the coals to the
kitchen stove and started the fire so Ma could make breakfast.

Because the houses we lived in were always drafty and cold in
winter, keeping the little ones in the family warm presented a
problem. To solve it Ma and Dad simply kept their bed in the front
room and the little ones slept with them. At one point along the way
we also had a little iron baby crib, painted white, where a toddler
slept while the nursing baby remained with Ma and Dad.

Another important piece of furniture in the front room was an old-
fashioned writing desk. The writing leaf had long since disappeared
but Ma still kept her writing tablet, envelopes, pencil and any
important papers in the little "cubby" holes at the top out of reach of
the younger children. The bottom drawers provided storage space
for socks and underwear.

Sitting close to the heating stove to provide a comfortable place to
rock the baby was our big wood rocking chair. And over near the
window where the light shone in for easy visibility sat Ma's most
useful piece of equipment, her treadle sewing machine.

The only other piece of furniture I can remember in our front
room was a table where the kerosene lamp sat. These tables, common in that era, were called stand tables. The legs were set at an
angle from the top past a slightly smaller shelf at the bottom ending
with glass-balled feet at the floor.

My brothers and I slept in the room which adjoined the front room. Because the rooms in older houses were quite large, the bedroom easily accommodated two or three beds. The metal beds, equipped with iron side rails and wood slats, were padded with mattresses made of straw-filled ticking. Ma made comforters using swatches of material from old wool coats and heavy denim work clothes, a layer of cotton or wool batting in the middle and a bottom layer of dark cotton flannel. With a heavy darning needle and colorful yarn when she had it, or just plain string saved from flour sacks, she ran through all three layers at regular intervals, then cut and tied them to hold the layers securely together. Because of their bulk and weight these heavy comforters were washed no more often than once a season. Therefore, Ma admonished us to keep muddy feet or food or anything that might soil away from the beds.

Ma fashioned sheets for our beds from flour sacks. Flour, one of our staples, came in 48-pound bags. When the cotton muslin bag was emptied and opened up, it measured about a yard square. We used a bag of flour every two weeks so Ma always had an ample supply of sacks to work with. Their use was not limited to sheet making. Ma made dishtowels, baby diapers, underwear and even kitchen curtains from these versatile bleached muslin flour sacks.

In our bedroom stood the only possession in which Ma took great pride. It was her good dresser. Made of solid, hand-rubbed walnut, it boasted a mirror that tilted. In it Ma kept baby clothes and her personal mementos and keepsakes. No one bothered Ma's dresser. I don't remember anyone telling us not to—we just knew it was special to Ma. It was the only thing of beauty in the house and Ma cherished it.

Once, late in the winter when it seemed that there was nothing in the house to eat and no money to buy anything, Ma received a post card from a recently married young couple. They offered to buy Ma's dresser for $5. She agonized over the matter. She knew we were out of food. She knew that no money would be coming in from furs nor any other source. It was a difficult decision to part with the only item of value in her life. But her children were in need of food. She would sell the dresser.

Quickly she wrote a penny post card and took it to the mail box and erected the flag for the mail carrier to see the next morning when he came.

A few days passed and the couple appeared at our home. They talked with Ma a little while. We wondered what they were talking so seriously about. It was simply this: The couple wanted the dresser. They didn't have the $5 they had earlier offered. They did have two one-gallon pails of sorghum molasses. Would she consider taking them in trade for the dresser? Ma's countenance dropped, then lightened. Yes, she would take the molasses in trade. It would mean the difference between hunger and survival for her family.

Molasses is a syrup made from the juice of sorghum cane cooked slowly until thick. It is rich in iron and energy. It is delightfully sweet. It is great for making popcorn balls, taffy, poured over pancakes or spread on corn bread. We enjoyed it. But we often wondered if Ma's beautiful dresser wasn't a bitter price to pay for two gallons of the sweet syrup.

In the wintertime Ma's greatest concern in our substandard houses was keeping the cold out; in the summer it was keeping the flies out. She poked rags in the cracks around the windows to shut out the wind in winter. The floors were cold even when the room temperature was comfortable. Once when Ma was seated behind the heating stove bathing my baby sister Shirley, as was her custom daily after the boys had gone to school and Dad had left to run his traps, she discovered the soiled baby clothes she placed on the floor were frozen in the short time it took to dress the baby and put her on the bed.

The very first thing we did in winter upon arising was to put our shoes on. The first person to get a drink of water broke the ice in the water pail.

In the summer, to combat the ever-present flies, Ma tacked cheesecloth on the windows for screens. If there were existing screen doors, she patched and repaired them to keep the unwanted flies outside.

The rough, unpainted pine-splintered floors bore no carpet nor linoleum. Dirt collected in the cracks making cleaning virtually impossible. Ma swept at least twice a day and scrubbed twice a week. Floor scrubbing followed clothes washing to make the maximum use of the short supply of water.

Without exception, in every place we lived the well was at least a quarter of a mile from the house, usually at the bottom of a hill. On washday, a twice weekly ritual, the boys carried enough water to fill the iron wash boiler. Ma removed the lids from the fire box of the cook stove which left an opening that allowed the boiler to fit in snugly. When the water came to a boil, Ma added enough lye to "break" the minerals and make the water soft. After she dipped off the mineral scum, Ma poured half the hot water into a washtub and cooled it down by letting white clothes soak in it while the boys filled the rinse tub. When the wash water had cooled just enough for her hands to bear, she began hand-rubbing each item on the washboard. One of us turned the rubber wringer with the hand crank to remove the soiled wash water from the clothes. Ma added the freshly rubbed items to the boiling water on the stove for whitening and sterilizing. After all the white boilables were finished, Ma washed the light colored clothes. She finished up with Dad's and the boys' overalls and work shirts. When all the clothes were washed and rinsed, Dad or the boys carried out the dirty water. Ma reserved the final rinse water to be heated for scrubbing the floors.

In the summer the clothes dried quickly in the hot sun. But in winter Dad strung up lines across the front room and kitchen so the heat from the heating stove and cookstove could evaporate the moisture from the heavy jersey long underwear and the thick denim overalls.

Ma made her own lye soap for washing clothes. The recipe had been handed down from her mother and her mother's mother. The basic ingredients were animal fat, lye and water. Chemically, the lye simply caused a hydrolysis of the fat. The actual process always seemed more mysterious. We viewed the boiling cauldron as a sort of witch's brew. We marveled at the way Ma could take dirty grease that normally would soil one's clothes, simply add lye and water to get a mixture that could be poured into boxes and cut into bars to produce suds-making soap.

When the wash was completed, next day came the ironing. Ma had two heavy flat irons which she heated on the cookstove. One removable handle was used to alternate from the hot unused one on the stove to the cool one just used for ironing. It took a lot of practice to learn how to assess the correct temperature for proper smoothing of the material without scorching a fine white shirt or blouse. Ma seldom scorched anything. To make certain the iron was heated just right, she held it in her right hand, stuck the second finger of her left hand to the tip of her tongue and then touched the hot iron quickly to determine the measure of heat. If a quick touch produced a hiss, the iron was ready for pressing. If not, Ma moved the iron over to a hotter spot on the stove for quicker heat induction.

To attempt to make a comfortable home from the low quality houses we lived in did indeed present a challenge. Over and over Ma proved that she was equal to the task.

Ma's Lye Soap Recipe

5½ pounds waste   1 can lye
   cooking fat   1 cup powdered borax
1 cup ammonia   1 ounce sassafras oil
Water   (optional)

A day before making soap, add the grease to water in a large iron or porcelain pot and boil to remove salt and foreign matter. When it cools, skim off fat.

Dissolve lye in three pints of hot water and cool to lukewarm. Remelt grease, add borax and mix well. Add ammonia and mix again. Now, add lye water to dissolve the grease. Add oil of sassafras to cut fatty odor and improve fragrance. Stir at least half an hour, and continue to stir until the soap begins to harden.

Pour soap into a cardboard box or metal container and keep in a warm place for two days. Cut lines across the top with a knife to make it easier to break into bars later. For best results, let soap stand for a couple of months before using.

Chapter Four

Corn Bread, Beans Hominy and Greens

Food was the essence of survival. We were constantly on the lookout for new and different sources of supply. We foraged for everything edible that the earth yielded. We searched the woods for wild greens, berries, mushrooms and nuts. My brothers hunted rabbits, squirrels, ducks and geese for meat. When we lived near a body of water such as a creek or pond, we fished for catfish, bullheads and carp. The boys speared bullfrogs for their tender meaty hind legs.

Ma had an uncanny ability to take the lowliest edible product and transform it into something delicious. Her ingenuity was often taxed to the utmost, particularly in the late winter months when home canned fruits and vegetables were in short supply and little or no fresh game was available. She baked "light" bread every other day. The aroma which emanated from her kitchen could easily have competed with any bakery.

"Light" bread was the name given to home-baked, yeast-raised bread. Interestingly, Ma never used commercial yeast. Each family maintained a "starter," so-called because it started the bread to rising. Each time she baked, Ma retained about a cup of the batter and placed it in a small brown stoneware jar, sprinkled a generous handful of sugar on top, covered it and put it in a cool, dark place until the next baking day. It was important not to allow the starter to get too warm and sour or to get too cold and freeze. On rare occasions when either happened, it became necessary to go to a neighbor and borrow some of her starter. Neighbors were happy to accommodate one another as it was not unusual for anyone's starter to fall prey to the changing household temperature.

Ma usually baked about six loaves of bread and a pan of sweet buns each time she baked. In addition, for a special treat, she often cut off pieces of dough and fried them in hot grease for after school munching.

Ma's grocery list consisted of flour, sugar, salt, dry beans, baking powder, soda, lard, coffee, vinegar and cocoa. Everything else we either did without or made ourselves. When she was out of lard she simply greased the bread pan with a meat rind.

For as long as I can remember we had skillet gravy and biscuits for breakfast, corn bread and beans alternating with fried potatoes and gravy for dinner and supper. Meat rinds added flavor to the beans. When we had canned greens, tomatoes, fruits or vegetables, they provided an added dimension. Meat of any kind was cause for celebration.

When we lived near our Grandpa and Grandma Sevits we could count on having milk. Because they sold cream instead of whole milk they always had an abundance of skim milk. Each milking time, morning and evening, Grandpa turned the crank on their DeLaval cream separator until he built up enough revolutions per minute to provide the centrifugal force to drive the cream up and over and down the spout into a cream pail, while the milk remained at the bottom and went into the skim milk pail. Grandma made cottage cheese with the skim milk after it had clabbered. She fed the remaining whey to the hogs. But we could have all the fresh skim milk we wanted to carry home. My brothers and I usually carried two one-gallon syrup pails full home each day. In winter the milk was frozen solid and in summer it was often sour by the time we arrived home with it. When the cows went dry, or when we lived away from our grandparents, we made-do without milk. Then Ma made our gravy and biscuits with water.

We all drank coffee even from a very young age. We delighted in a special treat which we called "coffee soup." To make it we placed a thick slice of bread on the plate, poured coffee over it and sprinkled sugar on top.

Corn bread was one of our favorite foods. We normally bought the white corn especially grown for corn meal and took it to the mill for grinding. An elderly man and his three adult sons were well known in the community for growing high quality white corn for meal. They were equally well known for their fear of snakes. Once Ma, Cleo and I borrowed Grandpa Sevits' team and buggy to go to the Ewings for white corn. The small corncrib, filled to capacity, required climbing a narrow ladder on the side to the top to get the corn. I was just a little girl but the idea of climbing the corncrib ladder fascinated me. I was half way up when young John let out a spine-chilling scream.

"Snake!" he shouted. Sure enough, there slithering along the side of the corncrib at just about the same level I had reached was a huge, harmless black snake. Ma, afraid of snakes, too, as most women are, shrieked in terror.

I was totally oblivious to all the furor. I didn't see the snake as posing any immediate threat to my life or limb because, to tell the truth, he was trying hard to get away. I thought old John was going to have a heart attack. Everyone was thrashing around with hoes and sticks and other hazardous tools, but luckily for the snake, he got away. I'm sure I was in more danger from a fall than from the snake.

Before we left and after everyone had calmed down a bit, Old John told us a story about a harrowing experience he had had with a snake earlier that season.

"I allow as to how the other night, a couple of weeks ago, a big storm came up. The sky got real dark and cloudy and the wind started blowin' hard. Well, I lit up my lantern, grabbed my walking stick and headed for the fruit cellar. Just as I went in the door, a gust of wind blowed out my lantern. And at that same instant, my eyes caught sight of a big black snake. Well, the wind was a howlin' and the thunder was a rollin' and I could not go out into that storm. But I was afeared of that snake. What was a body to do? Well, I sat myself down in the middle of the floor and all night long I tapped the floor all around me with my walking stick. I never slept a wink."

"What happened to the snake?" we asked.

"That's a mystery," Old John explained. "When morning came he was no where in sight."

Hominy, another year-round staple food, was also made from white field corn. Ma filled the iron boiler (the same one she used each week for washing clothes) about half full of white shelled corn, covered it with water and brought it to a boil. Then she added lye to loosen the hulls from the corn kernels. As soon as the hulls were loosened, she poured off the hot lye water to continue the cooking process with fresh water until the grains were plump and tender. Because hominy normally was made in the winter, Ma simply stored it in a big stone jar in a cool place and took out enough for a meal at a time.

As soon as winter passed and vegetation began to show along the creeks, we went searching for wild greens. Wild lettuce and dande-lion were probably the earliest varieties. Then came the cow weed, carpenter's square, lamb's quarter, sour dock and water cress, and later wild mustard. Wild onions added a little extra flavor.

Immediately following the wild greens came a true gourmet delight, wild mushrooms. We learned to recognize their sponge-like, little-evergreen-tree shape at an early age. Turned in flour and fried in a big black skillet, their delicate flavor would have tickled the palate of a king.

At just about this time in the season we began to enjoy fresh garden produce—lettuce, radishes, onions. All summer long we could count on practically every kind of vegetable from the garden.

Dad raised a big garden and Ma canned the surplus. Tomatoes were perhaps the easiest of all the vegetables to can. First, we picked a bushel or so of the most red ripe ones in the garden. I usually washed glass canning jars because my hands were just the right size to slide easily into the mouth of the jar. We heated enough water to the boiling point to cover the tomatoes to loosen their skins. We peeled each one, gave it a little squeeze to remove excess seeds, packed them firmly into the jars, added a teaspoon of canning salt and screwed the lid on tightly. This method was called cold packing. Then we placed the filled and sealed jars into the copper bottomed boiler, filled it with water to the shoulder of the jars and brought it to a boil. Tomatoes required only 30 minutes of boiling time but the kitchen could get quite warm on a hot late summer day even for that short period of time. When the cookstove was fired up for canning, Ma always put on a big pot of beans at the back of the stove to cook while the canning boiler was going full steam. Sometimes Cliff baked a cake if he could find the necessary ingredients. The oven could be counted on to stay hot for most of the day.

Later in the depression years when some of the assistance programs were initiated, county extension offices introduced women to pressure cookers for safer home canning. Most vegetables with high starch content were difficult to successfully preserve in the traditional cold pack method. Homemakers experienced a high ratio of spoilage to the number of quarts processed. The primary advantage of the pressure canner was that because higher temperatures could be maintained under pressure, the product was subjected to a shorter processing time, so that more vegetables could be canned in one day thereby catching them at their optimum condition.

One early August afternoon when Ma had been canning corn all morning, and had still another batch in the canner, a peddler knocked at the kitchen door. He was selling linoleum floor covering.

"Good afternoon, madam," greeted the salesman. "I can see I have come to the right place. I have something for you that will revolutionize your cleaning chores. I have a beautiful linoleum in my truck that would give you just the lift you need today. Am I right?"

"Of course, you're right, but I don't have a dime to my name to spend for a linoleum," Ma responded.

"Well, now," countered the salesman, "don't you have an old hen or some eggs?"

"Not one I could spare," replied Ma.

"I would trade for some of this lovely canned corn," he said and with that picked up a half-gallon jar which Ma had just taken out of the canner and had set on the floor for cooling. He had not been aware of the temperature of the jar. It was *hot*. Almost like a choreographed ballet, he danced back to the spot where he had picked up the blistering container and gingerly set it down. Relieved, but with scorched fingers, he continued to bargain. He would take four half-gallons of the corn and $2. Cleo, who was anxious for Ma to have the beautiful new floor covering, called her into the other room.

"Ma," he said, "I have $2 and I know how much you would enjoy a nice linoleum for the kitchen. Let's get it," he pleaded.

"All right," Ma reasoned. "I can't refuse an offer that generous."

Cleo helped the salesman bring the linoleum in from the truck and found four cool jars of corn for the trade. The linoleum was beautiful.

Its reds, greens and yellows truly brightened up the room and Ma's day. Cleo felt good about his contribution. We were all delighted with the new addition to our otherwise drab kitchen.

The joy the linoleum brought was short lived, however. The first time Ma scrubbed it, most of the color came off in the scrub water. It was nothing more than painted tar paper. There was no way to locate the salesman as he was not working for any established firm. We did learn a lesson in consumerism: Let the buyer beware.

Some vegetables and fruits lent themselves quite well to an extremely simple and economical way of preservation called dehydration. It was easy, because this method eliminated a number of work steps, and economical, because it eliminated the need for expensive containers. Besides, it took less wood and water.

Because green beans were so easy to prepare for drying, children were often given the assignment with little supervision. Early in the morning, just as soon as the sun had evaporated the dew, we picked the young tender green beans. The next step was to wash them and remove the ends. Then we threaded a large darning needle with heavy Number Eight thread, or string saved from the store and strung the beans up in about two-foot lengths, securing the end so the beans wouldn't fall off. Finally, we hung them up to dry either on a nail on the wall or draped over a wire stretched across the unused room. When they were completely dehydrated we stored them in an empty lard can with a tight-fitting lid to protect them from bugs and mice.

Drying corn was considerably more involved and entailed much more effort. Ma was pretty much in charge of this operation. The boys could go as early as they wished to gather plump ears of sweet corn because the dew didn't cause rust in the corn as it did in the beans. They gathered a flour sack full each. We all helped shuck and silk the golden ears. Then Ma and I, using sharp kitchen knives cut the corn from the cob, scraping the cob after each cutting to remove every morsel of edible product. Because of the high starch content, corn required preboiling to eliminate any possibility of the survival of spoilage-promoting bacteria. As soon as the big kettles of corn came to a boil, Ma stirred them to prevent scorching. When she was convinced they had boiled long enough to eliminate the fear of spoilage, she drained off all the liquid. Then Ma gave the boys enough clean muslin to spread on the shed roof to accommodate the corn for drying. Although the boys were in charge of the roof-top job, Ma climbed up high enough to supervise.

After the corn had been spread evenly on the muslin squares, the boys covered them with cheese cloth to keep flies from contaminating the corn. Naturally, this process called for a hot, sunny day. A hint of rain postponed corn drying to another day. Periodically the boys climbed back on the roof to inspect and rotate the corn to hasten the drying. In midwinter the delicately flavored cooked dried corn brought back memories of warm summer days.

We dried apples in much the same way except the cooking step was not needed. We simply picked and peeled the apples, sliced them and spread them on the muslin squares for drying. Because apples were harvested in the fall, the drying process took a bit longer. The apple slices grew brown because of their longer exposure to the air.

In the winter, Ma made delicious dried apple dumplings, a dish she learned to make from her mother. She stewed the dried apple slices and then added spoons full of dumpling batter. Steamed for a few minutes on the stove, the result was indescribably delicious.

Many rural people kept bees and harvested their own honey. Because we moved so much it was impossible for us to have bee hives. But Cleo and Cliff knew how to recognize a "bee tree" in the woods. When they located one, Dad went with them to harvest the honey. After donning long-sleeved shirts and heavy overalls, plus a protective cheesecloth headgear, they armed themselves with an axe to cut into the tree and a bucket and dipper for retrieving the golden honey.

In midsummer we began to search out the known berry patches and were always on the lookout for new ones. Blackberries, one of the most plump and juicy varieties, could be found along the railroad tracks. We found dewberries along the road sides and along the fence rows around the pastures. Strawberries were a bit more elusive, a special treat to be savored with delight when we did stumble upon them. Gooseberries were tart little round berries which we picked when they were green. They grow on thorny bushes scattered deep within the woods.

One day after we had tramped for hours picking the sour little berries and our muslin flour sacks were nearly filled, we were surprised by a man carrying a rifle.

He shouted, "Lay down those berries and get out of here!"

We couldn't believe our eyes. We knew that man. He was the father of one of our school friends. We responded, "You're only joking, right?"

"No, I'm not joking," he answered firmly.

We realized he was serious, so we put down our bags and trudged home. We were fully aware that we were on someone else's property, but no one ever cared if we picked berries or greens or mushrooms. There was plenty for everyone.

When we told Ma our story, she was furious. She could not imagine a grown man being so cruel. There would be no gooseberry cobbler at our house this day. She hoped his family would enjoy theirs.

In the fall, right after the first frost, we began to look for hickory nuts, walnuts and hazelnuts. Hickory nuts and walnuts grew on tall trees, but they normally fell to the ground and we simply picked them up. The problem was the outer husk. Walnuts were especially difficult because of the nearly indelible dark stain they left on hands and clothing. Ma always warned us not to eat the nuts until they had seasoned a few weeks. A severe belly ache was sure to be the consequence of eating walnuts and hickory nuts prematurely.

The hickory nuts which came from the hillside trees were tiny but the most flavorful. Another variety grown along the river bottom land were much larger, but not nearly so tasty. In midwinter a hickory nut cake or fudge topped with black walnuts were rare and welcome treats.

Hazelnuts grew on low bushes in clusters cloaked in paper thin outer husks. One large crisp chewy kernel occupied the easy-to-crack shell.

One of our neighbors even grew peanuts. One cold day shortly before Christmas, she came over to bring us a gift of her home grown peanuts along with a recipe to make molasses candy using the nuts for added crunch. Ma was anxious to try out the recipe, so as soon as our friend left, we all helped shell the peanuts. We didn't have to roast them first because the heat from the cooking candy would do the job.

It was a great recipe and it worked perfectly. All we had to do was wait a few minutes for the candy to cool After spooning the thick fudgy candy out into a big pan, Ma set it out on the back ledge to cool.

Excited and anxious to try out the new candy, someone quizzed, "Is the candy ready yet, Ma?"

"Yes," Ma affirmed, "it must be ready by now. Will you go get it, Cleo?"

"Sure, Ma," Cleo responded as he fled out the back door and to the ledge where the candy had been set to cool.

"Ma!" he cried, "it's not here."

Over near the shed with his paw against the pan sat Cleo's dog, Old Tony, gulping down the last of the peanut candy. It was a good thing Ma let us lick the spoon and cooking pan or we would never have known how that peanut candy would have tasted. Poor Old Tony—it made him sick.

George Miller, an elderly farmer who lived near Hazel Creek School, planted a large patch of muskmelons every year and sold them to his neighbors throughout the bearing season. But when the first frost came, he invited all the boys and girls who passed by his place on the way to and from school to eat all they could eat and carry home as many as they could carry to the rest of their family. At the end of the school day the pungent aroma of over ripe cantaloupes enticed us to the patch. We ate until we could hold no more and each of us carried as many as possible home to share the delightful treat with the rest of the family.

Mr. Miller was famous throughout the county for his fine melons. His farm was blessed with a particularly rich sandy soil near the creek, coupled with his innate ability to grow the best. We always admired his generosity. Furthermore, because we knew he would give us all we could eat at the end of the season, we never took any melons earlier without his knowledge.

Ma used every method she could think of to preserve food for the winter. In addition to canning and drying, some vegetables such as potatoes, squash, onions and carrots can be stored without any processing at all. They were simply stored in the fruit cellar in wooden barrels or boxes.

One season after reaping a bountiful harvest, our fruit cellar was filled to capacity. Dad had worked hard to reinforce the old cellar dug into the side of a hill. He had made a new door and shored up the sagging walls. But one night the temperature dropped several degrees below zero. The walls and door did not provide enough protection. All the root crops froze along with a sizable amount of Ma's canned goods.

The next winter the house we lived in didn't have a fruit cellar. Anyway, I don't think Ma would have trusted her hard work to an old fruit cellar, especially with last winter's memory fresh in her mind. This time she would store her canned fruit and vegetables upstairs under the beds. They were sure to be safe there. Anyone knows heat goes up, and that room was directly above the heating stove.

We were hit with still another severe cold snap that winter. One morning we were in the kitchen still shivering while our breakfast warmed us up, when Ma came running with the baby in her arms and cried, "Oh, Tom, just look up at the ceiling!" Red juice was dripping through the broken plaster just above the heating stove. Hurriedly they both ran upstairs. They could not bear the sight before their eyes. Most of the jars of canned goods had frozen and broken. When the room warmed up they started leaking through the floor and into the ceiling downstairs.

In the winter the boys hunted rabbits and in the spring they shot squirrels. We fried the young tender ones and boiled or baked the older ones. They bagged an occasional duck or goose in season.

When we lived close to a body of water, Dad and the boys fished. Once when the fishing was especially good on Blackbird Creek, they made a bountiful catch of bullheads. Dad helped the boys skin and clean the fish while Ma got the big skillet ready for frying them up for a feast. After the fish were salted and turned in corn meal, she dropped each one into the hot grease to fry quickly. What a meal! We were all seated around the table enjoying the crisp fried fish when suddenly Cliff started choking. Cleo calmly took a look down Cliff's throat and spotted a fish bone. Ma was frantic. Dad tried to calm Ma and keep the rest of us quiet.

Cleo quickly told Cliff, "Don't swallow and I'll be right back." With that he grabbed the pliers from the cabinet drawer, ran to the fence and cut a piece of wire just long enough to make a tweezer. He returned in seconds, steadily inserted the tweezer and extracted the bone from Cliff's throat. With the emergency under control, we continued to enjoy our delicious fish dinner.

Neighbors and relatives often gave us food items that were less palatable to them. For instance, when they butchered a hog they gave us the head or liver or the feet or tail. These things were no doubt nutritious, but I couldn't help wondering why no one ever gave us a pork roast or sausage or tenderloin.

Once while Cliff was in charge of housekeeping while Ma was in the hospital, someone gave us a hog's head. Cliff wasn't quite sure how one went about cooking a hog's head, so he simply put it in a big pot and put it on the stove and boiled it. There is some pretty succulent meat on the jowls of a hog, and even the tongue is edible, but Cliff forgot to remove the eyes. When he brought the platter to the table we were all aghast to see the eyes glaring at us in a fixed stare. After a good laugh when the initial shock subsided, we devoured the hog's head.

Ma really liked having a few laying hens and some young chickens for frying. But we seldom had a place to keep chickens at our run-down places. Besides, it was difficult to move chickens from place to place.

One spring she got 100 male baby chicks from the hatchery for two cents each. Because the hatchery sold pullets for breeding, the males became discards to be sold cheaply for quick disposal. Ma knew she would have a problem buying feed for them. But she had that all figured out. The welfare department disbursed surplus commodities. We had an oversize supply of cracked wheat which had been given to us for breakfast cereal. It really tasted like chicken feed and we couldn't eat it. That is where Ma got the idea to get the chickens.

Ma fixed up a nice little coop and the boys helped make a pen. At about six weeks of growth, they were feathered out nicely and had begun to put on weight. One night a thunderstorm came up and created a flash flood. The next morning Ma found her beautiful little white roosters huddled together in the coop, drowned by the sudden downpour.

Wild game was our chief source of meat. But one summer we thought we had acquired the ultimate source of meat supply. The United States Department of Agriculture had determined that many of the milk cows around the country were diseased. They made a concerted effort to check all the cows of owners selling milk or cream. When we lived on Mr. Sandry's place, he had a number of dairy cows grazing on the land where our house was located. One day the Agriculture Department men came and killed his best milk cow. As soon as they were out of sight we decided to try and utilize the meat. Dad and the older boys went down where the cow had been killed, skinned and dressed the carcass and washed it clean with spring water.

Ma and I washed canning jars and rounded up all the lids and rubber rings we could find. The younger boys carried water and by night fall we were ready to process the meat.

Dad was a skillful butcher. He cut the meat into chunks about two inches cubed. Ma and I stuffed the pieces in the canning jars, added salt and covered them with cold water. We sealed the jars up tight and placed them in the big copper boiler on the kitchen stove. All this we did by kerosene lamp light.

We worked as fast as we could, because we were acutely aware that spoilage was an imminent danger. But we were confident that our hard work would pay off. All night long the process continued. Finally when dawn broke, the four-hour boiling period had ended. There it was: A winter's supply of canned beef.

In less than a week the jars started spewing and a horrible odor emerged from their storage place. We failed, but God knows we tried.

It is difficult to understand how Ma and Dad were able to keep going in the face of so many failures. But the key to survival seemed to be that one never cried over spilled milk.

All our efforts were directed toward securing food to carry us through the winter. In spite of all the losses, somehow we always made it. And no matter how little food we had on hand, when a guest arrived, he was invited to eat with us.

We lived on the Albert Sullivan place during the drought of 1936. Where lush green grass had grown a month earlier, dust carpeted the front yard like talcum powder.

Ten-year-old Jimmy, his right arm carefully cradled in a freshly laundered, spotless white-muslin-flour-sack sling, ran as fast as his bare feet would carry him down the road from the mail box and across the barren front yard shouting, "Ma, they're coming. I can hear their car down the road a piece!"

Ma had made arrangements with Sant and Zulie, farm neighbors who went into town for trading weekly, to ride with them the 12 or so miles, to take Jimmy to the doctor for removal of the splint he had been forced to wear the past six weeks.

He had broken his arm in an ape-like leap from one branch in the big oak tree to another which turned out to be a brittle dead one. His action had been inspired by Alley Oop, the central figure in a new comic strip in the *Kirksville Daily Express*, portraying the antics of prehistoric cave- and tree-dwellers.

When the 1934, four-door Chevrolet sedan pulled up at the front gate, Ma and Jimmy wasted no time taking their places in the back seat. As the car moved steadily toward its destination, a trail of dust clouds spiraled behind it clinging close to the road, recording briefly the path it had taken.

Sant and Zulie, a middle-aged, childless farm couple, planned to spend the entire day when they made the trip to town for trading. Good neighbors, they were benevolent and kind, yet austere. Ma was fully aware of their habits and made her plans accordingly. They agreed to go their separate ways and to meet at four in the afternoon on the west side of the courthouse square to return home.

Earlier in the morning, just before sun-up, Dad had said to Ma, "Lulah, I'm up a gumstump this time; I know there has got to be water where we are digging, but so far we haven't hit it. If we just dig a few feet deeper, I know we'll find moisture." He had been helping a neighbor dig a well, but their earlier attempts had been futile. "Today will be different. I can feel it in my bones," he added. With that he threw the shovel over his shoulder and strode briskly down the dusty road, whistling as he walked.

Because we would be alone for the day, Ma had left my eldest brother Cleo, 15, in charge. She had started a pot of beans simmering on the back of the stove for our dinner at noon. She gave 13-year-old Cliff instructions to bring fresh water from the spring at the branch and to peel potatoes in the afternoon for supper. Milton, 11, was to cut wood for the fire and have six-year-old Robert help carry it in. I should wash the dishes after dinner and look after the little ones, Shirley, 3½, and Teddy, 1½.

The morning passed quickly as each of us willingly executed our assigned chores. We ate dinner early and the boys even helped with the dishes. Cliff went to the spring to get a bucket of water. While everyone else was busy, I coaxed Shirley and Teddy to lie down on Ma's bed and sang to them until they went to sleep.

Breathless from running up the hill with the water, Cliff excitedly exclaimed to Cleo, "The squirrels—were really barking—in those hickory trees. I'll bet we could kill—enough for a mess—for supper—if we took the rifle—and went right away!"

Equally excited upon hearing the news, Cleo replied, "Wouldn't it be great to surprise Ma and Dad with young fried squirrel for supper?"

Then he turned to me and asked, "Rene, would you be afraid to stay here with the little ones while Cliff and I go hunting? Milt could stay with you and help."

Pleased that my older brother had confidence in my ability, I responded proudly, "Sure, I can do it; don't worry."

As the two boys disappeared down the hill into the woods, Cleo toting the rifle as Dad had taught him, Milt took Robert outside to demonstrate the ancient art of hoop and paddle. It took patience, but soon Robert was guiding the hoop down the dusty road, keeping it centered on the paddle, preventing the hoop from running away.

While the little ones were sleeping, it occurred to me that I could bake a pie. I had watched Ma do it hundreds of times:

Make a well of flour in a deep bowl. Add some lard and water. Mix it together with your fingertips. The filling was just as simple. Cook the raisins. In a little glass bowl mix together flour and sugar. Add to the cooked raisins. Cook a little while until thickened. Roll out the pie dough. Put in the filling. Cut slits in the top crust to let the steam escape and pop it into the oven.

The recipe seemed simple enough. The only problem was there were no exact amounts. Amazingly, the crust turned out just right. The filling presented a far different story. As I had watched Ma mix flour and sugar together in a glass bowl, I had assumed she used equal parts of flour and sugar. I used a cup of flour and a cup of sugar. As I stirred the dry ingredients together and into the cooked raisins, the thickening grew stiffer and stiffer.

Unable to determine what I had done wrong, I hoped that baking the pie would somehow work magic and correct the problem. Undaunted, I scraped the doughy mess into the pie crust and with unrealistic expectations popped the pie into the oven.

The crust baked up to a golden brown, giving the outward appearance of a truly delicious pie. I was just setting it out on the cooling board when I was startled by Cleo and Cliff's animated conversation about the game they had bagged in their early after-noon hunt. Milt and Robert had given up their hoop paddling and had joined in the excitement. Curious to discover the reason for all the hoopla, I ran to find out for myself.

"What is it?" I cried.

"Well, it's a turkey," they responded in unison.

"A wild turkey?" I asked.

"We thought it was when we saw him scratching for food, but now we are not so sure," Cliff confessed.

"It could be one of Sant's tame turkeys," Cleo added.

Sant had the only tame turkeys in a 25-mile radius of our home. If it was a tame turkey, it had to be Sant's.

"Oh, Lord, what shall we do?" we incanted in unison.

With the truth out in the open, we had to make a rational decision. The harm had been done. The turkey was dead. We had no choice but to dress the bird and cook it for supper. We were not quite certain how Ma and Dad would view the error when they returned home. We would face that later.

The little ones were awake and up now. Milt brought in some fire wood. Cliff put the potatoes on. I set the table for supper. We began to watch and wait for Dad to return from well digging and Ma and Jimmy to return from town.

Dad came trudging up the path with his shovel on his back at about the same time Sant's Chevy stopped at the front gate. In a grateful neighborly gesture, Dad leaned the shovel against the porch, ambled up to the car, placed his foot upon the running board and his elbow on the car's roof, and said, "Howdy, Sant!" He continued, "Now I know you have had a long day and I'll bet you are hungry. Won't you stay for supper?"

Equally grateful for Sant and Zulie's kindness toward her and Jimmy, Ma joined Dad in the invitation, "We'd be proud to have you stay for supper, won't you please?"

Inside the kitchen, terror-stricken at overhearing the supper invitation, Cleo, Cliff and I tried desperately to find a way to conceal or disguise the turkey. Cleo and Cliff wished they could conceal or disguise themselves. Teddy and Shirley ran to meet Ma. We were afraid that they, in their infant innocence, would disclose the secret.

What seemed like endless ages passed until Sant replied, "We would love to have supper with you, but we have lots of chores to attend to, so we best get along home."

But Dad insisted, "Come on in. I don't know what the kids have cooked up, but it surely smells good!"

Inside we were praying silently, "Please, God, let their answer be a firm 'no'."

Zulie was final. She said, "We'll come back and have supper with you another time. Old Bossy just came fresh and she'll be miserable if we don't get home and milk her right away."

Sant patted Jimmy on the head and admonished, "No more Tarzan antics, all right, son?" And then he drove away. Ma and Dad waved goodbye.

When they came inside the kitchen, Ma went over to the stove, took off the lid from the pot the turkey was stewing in and asked, "Where did you get this big stewing hen?"

Nobody answered. Then everyone spoke at once. When the facts were all exposed, Dad and Ma agreed that under the circumstances we had done the right thing.

After a hard day's digging, Dad was starved. Having eaten a meager lunch on a limited budget, Ma and Jimmy were famished. Cleo, Cliff and I had lost our appetite in the anxiety, but with the relief following the confession, we were hungry, too.

We all ate as we had never eaten before.

"A fine supper, boys," Dad complimented. "And that was a pretty good raisin pie for a little girl's first attempt. With a little help from your mother, the next one should be even better," he added.

After supper our family entered into an unspoken covenant never to discuss our delicious secret, but we would remember it always.

Chapter Five

To Fetch a Pail of Water

If there was one central thread in the fabric of survival, it was the availability of water. The depression era embraced a period of continued drought throughout the country that created a multitude of problems, nationally and locally. For us the problem was reduced to two areas: finding water and carrying it home. We dug ponds and cisterns for catching rain water. We dug deep holes in the creek beds to collect water seepage from the sand. And there were the living springs, but they were always down over a hill, and the house was at the top. In the summer the water would be full of grasshoppers and warm when we reached the house. In winter, after slogging through the snow or slipping over ice, we arrived with frozen water.

There were all kinds of wells. Usually, each household had a cistern very near to the house situated so that rain water could be collected from the roof. A house must be equipped with an eaves-trough system in order to collect the rain water. Naturally, the substandard rental houses were seldom equipped with a rain water collecting system and the cisterns near the house generally posed a safety hazard because of the poorly constructed covers. When we lived at the Lee Mills place I recall little two-year-old Teddy delighted in poking the few table knives Ma owned through the cracks on the rough board top and listening for the splash as they hit the bottom of the contaminated water. Unless cisterns were cleaned thoroughly periodically they could not be used for household water, much less for drinking. So, if the cistern did function, its normal use was for dishwashing, cooking or laundry.

Because of the hilly terrain in northeast Missouri, living water was normally found in the lower levels, near a branch. Sometimes the water was simply allowed to collect in a scooped out natural rock formation. Spring water was always clear, crisp and cold, even in summer. If one was fortunate enough to have a natural spring on his land it was considered to be a great asset.

When we lived in the wooded hills west of Novinger on the Sandry place, these springs were quite common. The little spring-fed creek provided a delightful respite from the summer heat and dust. Oh, the joy of running barefoot through its shallow, cool water searching for Indian relics. The stones were clean and bright and always interesting. Now and then we found an intricately carved arrow. These were the times when we tried to imagine how a young Indian hunter stalked a rabbit or possibly a deer for his family's dinner. Oh, and could it be that these brightly colored stones once adorned a beautiful Indian maiden?

Once we stopped at Williams' spring to get a drink of their highly renowned supercold water. There, before our very eyes were two quart bottles with a rope securely tied around each neck, suspended into the cold spring water. We couldn't imagine what mysterious potion they might contain. We were even reluctant to tell Ma and Dad about it. But our curiosity won out and we did tell them. Ma and Dad laughed and said, "Don't tell anyone else about the bottles. You see, they contained homemade brew, and it is against the law to make beer at home."

Of course, we would not divulge a secret involving our friends, the Williams.

The natural rock-bound springs were a fairly rare phenomenon. In most cases when a land owner located a living water source, he proceeded to dig a deep well and lined it with rock or bricks and mortar, leaving the bottom open for the water to have a place to enter. Because the water source was usually remote from the house, it was especially important to provide a secure, safe top and a pump, if one could be afforded. If one was a bit more affluent, and particularly if there was livestock nearby to be watered, then a windmill became an excellent labor-saving device. In very rare cases, the windmill was utilized in even more energy producing ways. The windmill harnessed the wind power and transformed it into electricity through a home-owned generator. The homes which boasted a windmill powered generator usually had electric lights and a radio.

Dad located water with a device called a "divining rod." It wasn't a special tool bought at a hardware store, but rather self-designed and constructed from a forked, green elm branch. Dad walked along with the two forks in each hand and when the end pointed to the earth, there was a good chance water would be found. Dad dug a lot of wells in his time. Because the water vein was sometimes deep, the digging became hard work. But Dad always rejoiced with a wild "Yahoo!" when he finally hit water.

Our Grandma May's well was different from most wells I had seen. It was lined with smooth clay tile cylinders about two feet in diameter. The cover was a large heavy board secured by a heavy stone. To draw up water, one simply lowered a bucket on a strong hemp rope, leaned it over on its side and filled it to capacity and pulled it to the top. I had a morbid fear of falling in that well. I couldn't imagine how anyone could make a rescue.

Grandpa and Grandma Sevits' place was blessed with three sources of water. First, a clean, deep cistern right off the back porch supplied water for drinking, cooking and other household use. In the dry years of 1934 and 1936, after having several tanks of water hauled to refill the cistern from the city reservoir, they abandoned it in favor of the living well down over the hill.

Living water, because it filtered through rocks and minerals, was always "hard," while rain water collected in cisterns was "soft." Grandma didn't like the hard water but Grandpa liked it especially for drinking.

Even their pond, which was normally filled to overflow, nearly went dry during the drought. The pond provided water for the livestock and for laundry. Giving the horses a drink was quite simple. We just put a halter on each one and led him to the pond for a long drink before putting him in the barn for the night. But carrying water up to the house for the chickens or for laundry wasn't so easy. The hand-carved wooden yoke that Great Grandpa Felker had made years ago still helped to ease the load of two big water buckets. It fit snugly across the back and shoulders with two sturdy straps suspended on either side at arms' length for even distribution of the weight of the water. It always seemed a privilege to be allowed to don Grandpa Felker's yoke to carry water from the pond.

The deep wells and cisterns were a special concern for mothers for the safety of their little children. Little ones learned at a very early age to stay away from the well when anyone was drawing water. Occasionally the bad news arrived that someone's toddler had fallen into a well and drowned. Evidence from a crime was sometimes concealed in a well. And distraught persons took their lives in the deep recesses of the cool water.

But a good, clean deep well provided a more important service to households not equipped with any kind of refrigeration equipment. In the summer, milk, butter and other perishables were kept safe from spoilage in the cool wells.

Once when we lived in Sublette, Cleo took his last dime and bought the ingredients to make a batch of root beer. The recipe called for the soft drink to age for two weeks in a cool place. Naturally, Cleo chose the well. He found a bucket not in use, because of a hole in the bottom. He tied a piece of rope on the pail, and after he sealed the bottles, he placed them snugly in the bucket. Then he lowered the bucket to the point just above the water level for the two-week aging process. No one was allowed to disturb the aging brew.

At last, the appointed day for celebration arrived. As we all stood around the well top, eagerly awaiting a taste of the delightful drink, Cleo gingerly drew on the rope to lift up the bucket containing the bottles of root beer. The downfallen look on his face signaled that something was wrong. He continued to lift the rope until the end came. No bucket. The rope, weakened from the two weeks' suspension broke at the first tug. What a disappointment. We would probably never get to know how homemade root beer tasted.

If the summer droughts made the acquisition of water difficult, winter sometimes made it nearly impossible. In the winter of 1937 ice covered hill and vale for nearly two months. Getting water to the house and to the livestock was compounded by the slippery conditions. Ponds, of course, were frozen as well as the normal access to them. Dad helped the boys chop steps into the ice on the side of the hill going down to our well. They fashioned ice-grippers for their shoes from tin can lids by punching nail holes through to create a rough side to grip the ice. Under those conditions for acquiring water, we didn't waste a drop. We all washed our hands in the same pan of water throughout the day by simply adding a little fresh hot water from the teakettle each time. We saved all the waste water for the pig or chickens.

Washing clothes under ordinary circumstances was difficult at best. But when children got sick in the night the problem was compounded. One year there was an epidemic of scabies and impetigo in the school. Our family did not escape its wrath. When the county health officer examined our hands we were embarrassed to be told that we would have to stay home until the disease was cleared up. He sent a note home to Ma which read as follows: "Boil all bed clothes and wearing apparel. Come to my office in Kirksville as soon as possible for medication. The medication is to be applied after a hot bath every other day."

The next day Dad hiked into town to get the medicine. Ma organized the water-carrying and wood-cutting so the task of eradicating scabies could be completed at the earliest possible date. In constant succession, it seemed, she bathed and medicated each one of us. She washed and boiled clothes every day. In little more than a week, we were back in school, the epidemic contained.

In those trying times I learned that water was indeed a precious commodity. I learned to treat it with great respect.

Chapter Six

Hand-Me-Downs, Made-Overs and Patched Overalls

The clothes we wore were a monument to Ma and Dad's ingenuity. Ma remodeled and reconstructed hand-me-down garments and Dad repaired and restored shoes and overshoes.

One winter I was desperately in need of a warm coat. Someone had given Dad a long black heavy wool greatcoat. It had probably been stylish in 1920 but Dad had no place to wear such a coat. A double-breasted Chesterfield, it sported a beautiful black velvet collar. In Ma's mind's eye, she visualized a coat for me. Excited, she shared her idea with me. Eight years old, I couldn't share her enthusiasm over that old black coat.

The next day while we were in school Ma designed, cut and sewed. When we came home in the afternoon she met me at the door and said, "I'm just about finished with your coat. All I need is for you to try it on for length."

All I could see in *my* mind's eye was that horrible, long black greatcoat that Dad had refused to wear. Why should I have to wear it?

Then Ma came toward me with the coat she had made. I couldn't believe my eyes! The Sears and Roebuck catalog didn't have a specimen that could compete with Ma's creation. Oh, it was beautiful! Cut in a princess line, it was accented with the velvet collar, bound button holes and welt pockets. Absolutely no one in school wore a coat so beautiful. I was proud and so was Ma.

In addition to the coat, Ma made a pair of matching mittens from an ingenious pattern she had devised herself. Cut in one continuous piece the mitten could be sewed entirely on the sewing machine.

Although somewhat an expert at remodeling and reconstructing made-overs, Ma preferred to fashion garments from new material. On rare occasions when she sent in a mail order, sometimes Ma ordered a couple of yards of calico at ten cents a yard to have on

hand to make a new dress for me for a special school program or
church event.

She made shirts and trousers for the boys. They wore bib overalls
and chambray shirts, but special occasions called for them to look
their best.

Cleo had a leading part in the community play. He didn't own a
decent shirt. Dad hadn't sold any furs yet that winter so Ma couldn't
send off an order to Sears. What to do? Grandma Sevits had given
her a piece of tan silk pongee for a dress for herself which she had
made and worn before her last baby was born. It didn't fit now, so,
of course, it was stored away. She had planned to make herself a
blouse after the baby came, but somehow hadn't found time. It
would be perfect for Cleo's shirt. What about trousers? We had just
received a box of adults' clothes from our Aunt Opal, who with her
husband Ted lived in Las Vegas and worked in the gambling casino.
Because our Aunt Opal was "rich" according to our standards, she
wore chic, fashionable clothes. Generally these clothes were not
appropriate for Ma. Her alternative was to disassemble them and
reconstruct clothes for herself or me, or try and sell them to young
single girls in the community or trade them for some of their outgrown clothes for me.

Ma sorted through the box of clothes and found a dark brown
gabardine skirt. That would be just right for new pants for Cleo. She
carefully removed the zipper to be reused in the front fly. Again, she
worked like a wizard. Cleo was thrilled when she produced a neat
silk shirt with regulation reinforced neck and collar and trousers that
rivaled anything ready made.

"Why, Ma," Cleo marveled, "they have swinging pockets, just like
in the catalog!"

Ma's satisfaction came on the night of the play when everyone
remarked about Cleo's fine appearance and delightful performance.

Ma enjoyed creating attractive clothes for us. But her main task was
simply to provide covering for our bodies to protect us from the winter cold. If at all possible, we started the winter season with two pairs of
long knit underwear. Along about Christmastime, they began to need
patches. The knees had patches on patches by spring. Our homemade
mittens were either patched or replaced once or twice during the
winter. And socks always needed mending. Knowing that the knees
on overalls were the first to go, Ma took preventive measures and put
a patch on brand-new overalls, after they had been washed a time or two.

The need for shoes and overshoes provided a constant concern. Dad repaired the leather shoes on his shoe last and staff. Overshoe repair was quite different. Dad never owned a car, but he always had a tire repair kit. Tire patches provided the just-right equipment for repairing rubber overshoes. First, Dad located the hole. Next, he took the tin scraper provided in the kit and roughened the spot around the hole. Then he applied the rubber cement. Last, he peeled the backing from the red or green patches and stuck one firmly in place over the hole. There, good as new. True, the overshoes were again waterproof. But we thought the red and green patches made us look a little silly.

When Cleo was about 15, he had gone into Kirksville with Uncle Ted and Aunt Lola. They had parked down near the feed mill where Cleo noticed a sign advertising a rummage sale. Curious, he walked down the street and into the garage where the goods were displayed. He couldn't believe his eyes! There were beautiful white shirts, three for a dime. There were kids' clothes, dresses for Ma, shoes for the whole family—everything. He bought everything he could get with his $1.50, and the nice ladies threw in some extra things for good measure. They asked about his family and told him to tell his mother to come to see them the first time she came into town.

When Cleo got home and distributed all the great things he had bought for us, he told Ma how nice the ladies had been and that they wanted to meet her. Ma was pleased that these benevolent women were interested in her and her family, but pondered it with a grain of salt.

A few weeks later, she and Dad did have an occasion to go into town. Out of curiosity more than anything else, she decided to pay the rummage-sale ladies a visit. Because Cleo had bought something for each one of us at their sale, they knew all our sizes. They had accumulated several boxes of good wearable clothing and shoes for all of us. Ma was overwhelmed. "But you don't even know us," she protested.

"We learned a lot about the kind of family you have from your son's unselfish devotion to his mother, father, brothers and sisters," the nice lady said. "We have these rummage sales to raise money for charitable works. If that boy could spend the last penny he owned for his family, we could do no worse than to gather up some things that we could no longer use."

When Ma came home late that evening, we dug through the boxes by lamplight and basked in the glow of our newly acquired wealth. I remember especially a pair of black shiny patent leather Mary Jane slippers that were just my size. Along with them I found a pair of long white stockings. I couldn't wait for Sunday to come so I could swing my legs from the church pew and look just like the pastor's daughter who only last week had laughed at my "plow" shoes.

Not only did Ma sew for us, but friends whose children had grown up and left home, made clothes for us, too. Some did it simply because they wanted to do nice things for us. But some did the sewing for Ma when she was ill knowing that Ma would do the same for them when the need arose.

Ma believed in giving good care to the clothes we had. She insisted that we keep our best garment in a state of good repair at all times. We wore one outfit to school for a week, removing it in the evening and changing into our more tattered at-home clothes.

It is true that we owned very few purchased garments. Our clothes were often shabby. But we always looked our best in public. Ma made certain of that.

Cliff, Cleo, Milton and James in overalls, baby
Shirley, Roena and Robert in made-over
hand-me-downs

Chapter Seven

The Crying Times

Hardship was truly a way of life, but it never was an adequate preparation for the human tragedies that befell almost every family we knew, as well as our own. Nearly every winter friends or relatives lost children to communicable diseases like scarlet fever, measles or whooping cough and their complications.

In the winter of 1937, a severe one complicated by thick ice cover making travel difficult, an epidemic of scarlet fever ran rampant throughout the community. The disease, characterized by high fever and red splotchy rash with subsequent peeling skin, was highly contagious. When a family was stricken with any of the communicable diseases, the county health officer promptly tacked a quarantine sign on the door warning others to stay away. The occupants of the home were equally warned not to leave the home to mingle with others for any reason. In the case of some diseases such as chicken pox, measles or whooping cough, the adult members could go to their jobs or socialize in any way they chose. But the children were totally confined to their home. In the case of scarlet fever, however, neither adult nor child was allowed to mingle with any other persons. It was believed the germs could be carried on clothing or in the air. To prevent contamination, it became necessary for good neighbors whose family had already had the disease, to bring supplies to the stricken family. Of course, they were not permitted to come into the house.

Dee and Emma Van Laningham's family fell victim to the disease that winter. Simple people, they lived by a creek near the coal mine where Mr. Van Laningham worked. The children all came down with the dread disease. The older ones came out of it with no complications, but Dee and Emma lost their two youngest. It is difficult to imagine a sadder scene than the burial for those little innocents. No one was allowed to come for a public funeral. The only persons present were the men who dug the grave, Mr. Van

Laningham and the minister of the church. They were all obliged to
wear clothing they could afford to discard, because following the
graveside service, their outer garments were burned.

My own little month-old baby brother died that winter, too. Born
on January 10, he developed pneumonia when he was just about
three weeks old and died in Dad's arms on the night of February 9. I
can see it yet. Ma called Dad saying, "Tom, come quick! Little
Franklin isn't breathing very well." Dad tenderly picked up baby
Franklin Delano, named proudly for our president, Franklin Delano
Roosevelt, carried him over near the lamp and close to the warmth
of the heating stove. Placing his head close to the baby's chest, Dad
listened carefully. Then he held our little brother up in front of him, it
seemed just to look at him once more. Little Franklin gave a weak
sigh, accompanied by an angelic smile and he was no more.

Ma's best friend, Rosie Yadon came at once, bathed and dressed
our little dead baby in preparation for burial. Early the next morning
Dad and Uncle Ted drove to Greentop to purchase the tiny white
casket for the funeral. Cleo gave Dad the necessary $10 as a loving
memorial to our little brother. He had saved the money from working in the hay the summer before.

As children, I don't think we were grief stricken. It was just a
mystery. Why was our sweet, innocent little baby taken away? But
Ma wept at the slightest provocation. Her tears came from profound
grief, but she was gravely ill at the same time. She became weaker
and weaker. Finally when she became bedfast, Dad called the
doctor to the house. The doctor arrived at his diagnosis swiftly. She
was suffering from advanced infection resulting from childbirth.
She must be taken to the hospital in Kirksville immediately for
surgery. He could make no promises. Her condition was critical.

Dad lost no time in making arrangements to get her into town to
the hospital. The surgeon gave him very little hope for Ma's survival.
"We will operate and do the best we know how. That's all we can
promise," said the surgeon, matter-of-factly. "If she has a strong will
and an even stronger constitution, maybe she'll make it," he added.

Dad was dumbfounded. He had always pretty much taken Ma for
granted. Sure, she had suffered difficulty in delivery of her babies,
and yes, she had been ill from time to time. But for the doctor to paint
such a grim picture—Dad wasn't ready to hear that.

Grandpa Sevits advanced the $100 needed for the surgery and the
hospital stay. Dad had no idea how he would ever be able to repay it.

But he knew he didn't have to worry about that now. He was consumed with concern for Ma's well-being.

Then, of course, there were the kids at home. Cleo, 16, had just entered the CCC Camp. Cliff, 14, was placed in charge of running the household. Teddy, barely two, was still in diapers; Shirley, not quite four, needed lots of attention, too.

The rest of us ranging in age from six to 12 were assigned regular housekeeping duties. We carried water, washed dishes, peeled potatoes, chopped wood and helped with the little ones. Cliff washed clothes, cooked the meals and supervised the care of Teddy and Shirley. He maintained discipline among the rest of us in Dad's absence.

Days turned into weeks and finally after nearly a month, Ma came home. She was thin and pale. Little Teddy was frightened of her. Although we thought we had been doing a good job of running the house, Ma began to pick up and move things around.

One day, shortly after she had returned home, the boys and I decided to take a splash in the creek. It was mid-April—much too early for playing in the creek. Ma conjured up visions of all of us with pneumonia. Faintly we heard her calling to us, "Come back here at once! You'll catch your death of cold!" We should have known better. When we got back to the house Ma had collapsed across the bed. We helped her to lie down more comfortably. When Dad came home he called the doctor. The doctor ordered her back into the hospital. She stayed in for another two weeks. But this time when she was released, the doctor would only do so on Dad's promise not to return her to her family. Instead she must spend the summer staying with various relatives who would care for her in their homes.

That was the longest summer any of us could remember. Ma gradually regained her strength and we all grew up a bit faster.

Ma had not totally recovered when word came that her dearest friend and neighbor, Rosie Yadon had taken her own life with rat poison. Ma had been through a lot of suffering and she even said she could understand why Rosie would consider such a move. But, still, Ma felt even with all its hardships, life is precious. She grieved openly the loss of her dear friend. We missed Rosie, too.

When illness struck, neighbors rallied around and did whatever they could to lighten the burden for the stricken family. Fat and Omie Scott and their two daughters Lorene and Lois, lived in a two-room house next to the church. "Fat" was a nickname for a big man whose true name I never knew. Their whole family loved to eat and were all heavy-set. One day when Lois refused to eat and took to her bed, Omie knew her daughter was ill. The doctor was summoned to the house, who in turn diagnosed her illness as the flu. Omie was relieved to learn that Lois' illness was something as temporary as the flu.

But after a couple of days her condition worsened rather than improving as they had expected. She wouldn't eat, her temperature had accelerated, her breathing was labored and she seemed incoherent. The doctor came again. This time there was no doubt. Lois had pneumonia. Someone must sit with her day and night. They must give her alcohol-rub baths regularly to keep the fever down. Extra wood would be needed to keep the house warm day and night. There must be constant humidity in the house to aid in breathing. This meant the teakettle must boil constantly to provide the steam.

Lois lay in a coma for many days. Neighbors took turns sitting up with her, rotating on the night and day shifts. They took the laundry home with them, brought in food and helped with all the duties around the house, including chopping wood. Medical students from the American School of Osteopathy in Kirksville also kept a vigil along with the good neighbors.

Finally, the long hours of waiting and caring paid off. Lois came out of the coma. Her fever dropped and she asked for food. Everything would be all right now. Fat and Omie and the whole community rejoiced.

Some families were not as fortunate as the Scotts. Sometimes the tranquility of the community was interrupted by a violent accident ending in tragedy.

Warren Glaspie, a young daredevil, at 17 decided he could win some money riding a bronco at the rodeo in Waterloo, Iowa, where he was staying with his older brother. He approached the manager of the rodeo in his inimitable self-confident way and stated quite matter-of-factly, "I'm a cowboy who ain't never been beat by any horse. I think I can ride your wildest bronc."

The manager looked at him with a fatherly eye and answered, "You're a little young aren't you, son?"

"Whatta ya mean, young?" retorted Warren. "I'm 20 years old my next birthday," he added, stretching the truth.

"Have you ever been in competition before?" the manager queried.

CONNELSVILLE YOUTH KILLED AT EL PASO

Richard Sevits In Truck Which Hit Cotton Pickers.

Richard Sevits, 22, of Connels-ville, was killed yesterday at El Paso, Texas, when a truck in which he was riding with some soldier crashed into a group of negro cotto pickers.

He was the son of J. H. and De lie Sevits and had been working a store at Ottumwa, Ia., until cently. He went from Ottumwa California. Members of the f ily said he had received orders f Selective Service officials to re

Sherman Sevits Baby Dies Here

Charles O'Dell Sevits, 19 months old, died in a hospital here last night after being ill two weeks from cholera infantum.

The baby, son of Sherman and Maude Sevits, 503 North Baltimore Street, had been improving steadily the past few days. Under hospital care for several days in the first week of his illness, he was so much improved Sunday the parents were permitted to take him home. He became worse yesterday and had to be returned to the hospital.

The child was born on a farm east of Greentop. The family mov-'d to Kirksville when Mr. Sevits be-came secretary of the Adair County Farmers Mutual Insurance Co.

Surviving are the parents, three brothers, Wallace, 16; Willis, 15, and Harold, 11; paternal grandparents Mr. and Mrs. W. E. Sevits, Novinger and maternal grandmother, Mrs. G W. Willis, Greentop.

The funeral i...

Warren Glaspie, 17, Ia. Dies at Waterloo, Ia.

Funeral services for Warren G. Glaspie, who died Wednesday morning at a hospital in Waterloo, Ia., will be held Saturday afternoon at 2:30 o'clock at the Hazel Creek Church northwest of Kirksville Burial will be in the church ceme tery.

Young Glaspie, who was only 1 years of age, died from pneumoni He had been traveling with a rod company for the past three mont as a cowboy. He was the son Mr. and Mrs. Frank Glaspie w live northeast of Novinger. mother and a brother, Delbert Gl pie, were with him when he died

Besides his parents he leaves following brothers and sister: lie, of Hurdland; Willard, Marsl town, Ia.; Delbert, Worthin Mo.; Wallace, of the home, and John Waggoner, of near Fe One sister preceded hi 'tore. ath.

MISS LENORA DOLAN KILLED BY AUTOMOBILE

Miss Lenora Dolan, age 18, was fa-tally injured Wednesday morning about 8:20 o'clock when she was struck by an automobile on Highway 6 a short distance west of the point where Novinger's main street con-nects with the highway.

Miss Dolan and her brother, Wil-liam, had spent the night here and were returning to the home of their parents, Mr. and Mrs. Patrick Dolan, three miles west of here in the Bald Knobs community, when the tragic accident happened. They were walk-ing west on the highway, when W. J. Sandry, a neighbor, who was driving from the Farmers' Co-op. to Truitt Bros. Garage, saw them and turned west on the highway to talk to Wil-liam Dolan about working for him. When Sandry overtook the sister and brother, he stopped, and after a brief conversation the boy and girl turned to go, when another car, also traveling west, approached and start-ed around Sandry's car.

The headlines say it all

"Sure, I rode in Colorado and Wyoming," said Warren, trying hard to keep his myth alive.

"O.K., boy, it's your choice. The entry fee is $10; you got it?" the manager asked doubtfully.

"Yep, I got it right here. Won it in my last show," affirmed Warren as he handed the man two five-dollar bills.

"All right, here's your number. Go over behind that fence and wait your turn," replied the manager, shaking his head as he spoke.

Warren strolled over behind the fence, adjusted the number on his back and waited for his call. One by one the coyboys left the gates on their high-spirited horses, and one by one their times were read to the crowd. Warren knew he could beat their best time. He was sure he could stay on longer than any of the others.

Then the call came over the loud speaker: "Warren Glaspie, Number 42. From Colorado and Wyoming. Riding the meanest, orneriest cayute around. Give him a hand!"

The crowd cheered. The gate burst open. The horse lunged forward. Up he went and down he came, with Warren riding like a pro, smiling and hanging on for dear life.

Then the inevitable occurred. Warren's inexperience and over-confidence proved to be unequal to the horse's ferocity. With one violent buck Warren was thrown up in the air. He came to rest on the earth with a resounding thud. He lay motionless. The rodeo clown rushed to his aid. Warren could speak. He was conscious. But he was seriously injured. The ambulance screamed on to the arena. The attendants scooped up Warren's limp body and sped away to the hospital. In a matter of hours he developed pneumonia and in a few days he was dead.

They brought his body back to our little church for the funeral. His was the first funeral I had ever attended except for my baby brother's. He looked so bizarre. His face was covered with orangey makeup; his eyebrows were penciled and he was wearing lipstick! Somehow I tried to remember our great entertaining friend who wasn't afraid to ride his bike down the big hill tied to the back of a car or who dived from the tall tree over the swimming hole on a dare from the other boys. I tried to forget the painted figure lying in the casket. I closed my eyes and remembered him laughing.

Richard Sevits, our cousin, was his parents' only son. They had two older daughters, but he was the apple of their eye. He was handsome, dutiful, everything a good son should be. But he was 22 years old and out of a job. There were no jobs in Connelsville where he lived, nor in Novinger or Kirksville. He had been working in a store in Ottumwa, Iowa, but he was barely making enough to pay room and board.

One day he announced that he was going to hitchhike to California to look for a job. His older sister lived in San Diego and her husband had a good job in a defense plant. Maybe he could help Richard get a job.

Reluctantly, his folks agreed. Aunt Dollie, trying to force back the tears, packed all his belongings in a big black leather grip. She had patched his overalls and sewed buttons on all his shirts. She put in soap, his razor, wash cloths and towels. She hugged him passionately. She didn't want him to go. But she accepted the fact that he was a man and must make his own decisions. Uncle Jake, a man who seldom revealed his emotions, was noticeably moved by the leaving of his son. He put on a facade of anger to hide his sorrow. "This is all Roosevelt's fault," he exploded. "If it wasn't for all this damn war talk, our boys wouldn't have to leave home to find work."

Early the next morning Uncle Jake drove Richard over to Kirksville to the junction of the two main highways to catch a ride heading toward California. Uncle Jake shook Richard's hand. But then he lost all composure, threw his arms around the boy and cried bitter tears.

"Take care of yourself, son," admonished Uncle Jake. "And write to your mother and me, ya hear?"

"I will, Dad, don't you worry. I'll be all right," assured Richard.

With that, the two men parted, the young man eager, the older man sorrowful.

After several days Richard arrived in San Diego. He went down to the defense plant every day, but there were more job applicants than jobs. At 22 and with no job, he became a prime candidate for the draft. In no time at all, it seemed, he received his notice to report for induction.

He decided to return home for one last visit with his folks before reporting for active duty. He repacked his bag and headed back east, hitchhiking as he had come.

Two days passed and Richard was nearing the state of Texas. He had slept overnight with a nice family who had sent him on his way refreshed and ready to start on the last leg of his trip home.

Even though the hot, Texas sun had reduced the asphalt highway to soft, sizzling goo, Richard was confident as he waited. He was beginning to feel a little bit low when a truck filled with soldiers pulled over and offered him a lift. He was surprised, but glad.

"If you don't mind riding with dogfaces," shouted the driver, "climb in."

Did he mind? Not at all! His draft notice almost made him a soldier, too. Besides, he had a lot of questions to ask them.

Richard really enjoyed the company of his new-found friends. They exchanged stories about their home towns, the world situation, their girls back home and all the other things that young men talk about. Time was flying. They were making great time rolling along the highway.

Then it happened. With a crunch, a grind, breaking of glass and screams of fear and pain, two vehicles collided. In a matter of seconds it was all over. Richard lay bleeding. He was dead.

Uncle Jake remained bitter for years. He blamed Roosevelt's soldiers for killing his son. Aunt Dollie wept for the boy she would never hold in her arms again.

Sickness, injury, loss of property and even death brought immeasurable heartaches to the simple folks of our acquaintance, but they and we drew strength from each other. We cried, but there were times for joy, too.

Chapter Eight

The Good Times

Of all the simple pleasures that contributed to our good times, none remains so vividly etched in my memory as the times when Dad played the fiddle.

In the evening after Jimmy, Milton and I had finally bickered our way through the supper dishes, Dad took down his fiddle, went into the kitchen, perched himself on the stool chair, ran the bow back and forth through the chunk of resin, plucked the strings for tuning and then began to play. Sometimes he sang along. "The Strawberry Roan," the tale of a wild mustang, was one of his favorites. But we loved "Knocking on the Door," and "Pop Goes the Weasel." There were musical phrases in each of these tunes played pizzicato. We didn't know that the plucking sound he made was called by that name, but we were the only ones at school who understood what the teacher was talking about when she described pizzicato in music class.

While Dad played "Leather Breeches," "Arkansas Traveler," and "Turkey in the Straw," the rest of us occupied ourselves in pleasant constructive activity. I rocked the baby in the big rocking chair. The boys played checkers or cards while Ma patched socks or read the paper seated very close to the kerosene lamp.

Not only did Dad play the fiddle at home for his and our enjoyment, but he played for square dances, too. Sometimes when the weather was nice, and if the dance was in walking distance, the whole family went along. As we walked home in the moonlight the older boys helped carry the little ones who had long since dozed off to sleep.

Two of Dad's brothers played fiddle and banjo, too. On Friday and Saturday nights and Sunday afternoons in good weather, our uncles and others Dad knew who played harmonica, mandolin or guitar showed up at our house with their families to play and sing and simply enjoy the fellowship. They brought cookies, a pie or cake,

Dad and his beloved fiddle

popcorn or something that could be shared by all. Ma provided
plenty of hot coffee. When the number of pickers and singers and
the accompanying listeners outgrew an ordinary household, then the
hoedown was moved to the outdoors or to the district schoolhouse if
the weather threatened.

Exhibition of talent and sharing it with others seemed to be a
natural experience. Cliff and Cleo, when they were about 12 and 14,
went from school to school to pie suppers and talent programs
singing their repertoire of songs. Their most requested songs were
the ones with poignant messages.

"My Grandmother's Old Arm Chair," a perennial favorite, told a
story of initial disappointment followed by a pleasant surprise. The
gist of this story-song was that all the family members except the one
singing the song received great treasures in the disposition of the
grandmother's will. The singer received nothing except an old arm
chair. And, then one day while he was relaxing in the old chair, the
bottom fell out revealing thousands of dollars.

"Vicksburg Jail," another bittersweet tale related the story of a
young man and the agony he suffered after he had brutally mur-
dered his sweetheart.

They sang Dad's old favorite, "The Strawberry Roan." But their
most often requested song was "The Eastbound Train." This song
told the story of a little girl who had stowed away on a passenger
train to go to visit her blind father in prison, and of the conductor's

compassion when he assures the little girl that she will never need a ticket, while he is on the train.

"May I Sleep in Your Barn Tonight, Mister," another favorite, addressed itself to the many tramps and hobos who were common around the country.

They sang songs they learned from Ma, too. Her favorites included "When It's Lamplighting Time in the Valley," "Berry Picking Time," and a number of church hymns. Sometimes, if an organ was available, Ma joined them playing harmonic chords.

Cleo and Cliff didn't receive pay for their appearances. But they enjoyed the evenings out, meeting other young people and besides, there were always refreshments.

When a couple got married everyone looked forward to the charivari, commonly called a "chivaree." Weddings were simple, performed by a justice of the peace or minister in the parlor of their homes. No one ever thought of honeymoons or traditional receptions. But the community did get involved in the celebration of the wedding.

The men were always trying to invent some new ridiculous trick to play on the groom. They put rocks in the conjugal bed. Or they forced the groom to push his bride around the house in a wheelbarrow. Or they took the shades down from the bedroom windows and hid them. Or they even took the groom, fully clothed, and dunked him in the muddy pond. These asinine tricks were slightly sadistic but the couple dutifully submitted themselves to the stupid pranks to fulfill their role in the predestined drama.

And after submitting to the nonsense, they graciously distributed treats for all the well-wishers. A box of chocolates or a case of soda pop distributed amoung them appeased the crowd.

And then the dancing began. If the men seemed to make an inordinate number of trips out behind the smokehouse, it was because some enterprising fellow had acquired a bottle of brandy to celebrate the occasion.

The first snowfall of any measurable depth signaled good times sliding on the gentle slopes. A few of the older, more affluent young men owned toboggans or bobsleds. We contented ourselves with homemade sleds equipped with wood runners. Cleo, adept at cutting runners so they had just the right curvature, made our sleds. He shaped the runners from blemish-free boards with a wood plane and sandpaper. Then he added pieces across the top to sit or lie on. A bob-

sled required fashioning two jointed sections with a steering appara-
tus in front.

All the young people gathered early on a Sunday afternoon or at
night if the moon was bright. They made repeated trips up the hill
pulling the sled behind them, and then down with cheers and laugh-
ter. When the fun of sliding finally ended, everyone came inside for
hot cocoa and cookies.

One or two families owned horse-drawn touring sleighs. To see
them gliding by on a Sunday morning on their way to church and to
hear the jingling sleigh bells was reminiscent of a Currier and Ives
print.

Actually, farmers used sleds to take feed to their livestock in
remote pastures and to haul water or wood to the house. Just about
every farmstead had a working sled.

Winter provided the means for quite another recreational activity.
Nearly every boy over ten years of age could ice-skate. By the
middle of December most ponds and creeks were frozen hard
enough to sustain skaters. My brothers and their friends loved to
skate and play their version of hockey, which they called shinny. The
equipment for the game included a stick fashioned from a naturally
bent sapling tree and a tin can. They made up their own rules as they
went along and played simply for fun. There were neither winners
nor losers—everyone played.

One January Sunday afternoon, our cousin Wendell had invited a
number of friends and relatives to a skating party on the river near
his home. Cleo, Cliff, Milton and Jimmy went to spend the afternoon at the party. The three older boys owned clamp-on skates
which they had either purchased or traded from someone who had
outgrown them or who had recently bought rarely seen shoe skates.
Eleven-year-old Jimmy could only watch. He had no skates. Cousin
Wendell told the boys he had a pair of outgrown skates he would sell
for a quarter, 25 cents. Jimmy knew Cleo had a quarter he had
earned from selling rabbit hides. He started bugging Cleo to buy the
skates for him. Feeling a bit of guilt and obligation, Cleo made
Jimmy an offer: "I tell you what I'll do. If you can learn to skate
before the day is over, I'll buy the skates for you."

Well, Jimmy buckled the skates on to his shoes and got to his feet.
Down he went. He got up again and again until before long he was
gliding along as well as the older boys. Cleo knew he'd lost the
wager. But he was proud of Jimmy's skating. He couldn't wait to get

back home and tell Ma and Dad how quickly Jimmy had learned.

Jimmy truly mastered the art of skating. That same winter ice covered the earth from Christmas time until the end of February. On skates one could travel all across the countryside with ease. One day Jimmy and I were the only ones going to school from our family. Jimmy wore his skates and I held on to his hand. The road, rough from wagon and auto tracks, made skating difficult. We decided the going would be smoother inside the fence in the pasture.

"This is much better," we both agreed.

We were sliding along oblivious to the deep ravine below us, when suddenly Jimmy lost his footing and we started slipping down, down the deep ice-covered hill. We finally came to rest at the foot of a huge set of tree roots dangling from the bank of the ditch at the bottom of the slope. The top of that hill could not have appeared more remote than the top of Mount Everest. We were cold and frightened. When we gathered our wits we decided on a course of action. Jimmy would use his skates to cut footings in the side of the hill and we would climb carefully, hanging on to branches, bushes or whatever we could grasp to get us back to the top.

We struggled for what seemed like endless ages. Finally, exhausted, we reached the top. We had no idea what time it was, but we knew it was too late to try and go on to school. We sat down and ate our lunch and then headed for home.

When we arrived home earlier than usual Ma asked, "What are you doing home in the middle of the afternoon?"

After telling of our harrowing experience, we expected to be comforted. Instead, we were sharply reprimanded for doing such a foolish thing.

Some of the activities we engaged in for pleasure were often the source of great consternation to Ma. One Fourth of July Ma and Dad decided to take the two little ones and go to the annual picnic celebration. They really needed an opportunity to visit with adult friends and to get away from home for the change of pace. But they didn't want to enjoy themselves at our expense. Ma baked chocolate cream pies for our special treat and Dad gave the boys a good supply of penny firecrackers he had bought earlier just for today. Penny firecrackers, so-called because they sold ten for a penny were tiny and relatively harmless.

Ma felt uneasy about leaving us but Dad convinced her they need not feel guilty leaving school-age children alone for the afternoon.

Reluctantly, Ma bade us good-bye. As they walked down the dusty
road Ma pushed Teddy in the Taylor Tot stroller and Dad carried
Shirley.

They were scarcely out of sight when the wheels of our imagination began to turn. Cleo took his drill and bit and drilled a hole in the
end of a stick of firewood. Then he took the powder from a couple
of shotgun shells. He tamped the powder firmly into the opening in
the stick of wood and inserted one of the penny firecrackers for a
fuse. Then he called out to Cliff, "Bring Ma's washtub over here by
this tree."

Together they placed the homemade firecracker under the tub, lit
the fuse and ran. Ka Boom! What a Fourth of July spectacle! We
were sure they wouldn't have anything half as grand at the celebration. What went up in the air as an ordinary galvanized metal flat
bottomed washtub, had come down resembling half a large watermelon. There would be no way to explain this action to Ma.

To put the matter out of our minds, we went into the kitchen to
sample our chocolate pie. Cleo cut the luscious wedges of creamy
chocolate pie piled high with snow-white meringue, as we encircled
the table watching his every move.

At that moment, perhaps possessed by some evil power, one of us
put a penny firecracker in his pie, lit the fuse and laughed with satanic
glee while the chocolate filling exploded into a creamy cocoa mist
above the kitchen table. Obviously the situation was out of control.
Cleo arranged a whole package of ten of the penny firecrackers in a
circle, like candles on a birthday cake. Once lit, the effect was even
more spectacular than he had imagined. Chocolate pudding splat-
tered everywhere.

Memory has a merciful way of erasing some of the unpleasant
thoughts from the past. None of us recalls what consequences we
were required to suffer as a result of our unorthodox behavior. I can't
imagine the disbelief Ma and Dad must have experienced when they
returned to such a melee.

Daredevil antics were an integral part of our fun times. Some of
our friends, especially the boys, were even more daring than we.
Warren Glaspie was probably the best known daredevil in the whole
Hazel Creek community. Everyone liked to tell the story of the time
they were all swimming in the Jim Newcomer hole in Hazel Creek.
Someone dared Warren to climb to the top of a scraggly willow tree
which jutted out over the creek below and dive into the swimming

hole. Always eager to take a dare, Warren casually climbed to the top, flexed his muscles, took a bow and gracefully leaped with Olympic precision. The landing was not so graceful. His head penetrated the gooey mud at the bottom of the hole leaving his feet sticking straight up, as if he had been planted in that position. All the other boys ran to his aid, but in vain. He had already wriggled himself free and was on his feet taking a bow. A great cheer went up. No one doubted for a minute that Warren could pull it off.

Warren was one of the first persons we knew who owned a bicycle. The bicycle, more than simple transportation, was a source of thrills for Warren. The road that ran by our house at the Lee Mills place began at the top of one steep winding hill, ended abruptly at the bridge over Hazel Creek at the bottom, and then ascended sharply to another red clay peak. Warren, the only guy brave enough to ride his bike wide open down that hill and up the other, was preparing to outdo himself. He planned to tie his bike to the bumper of a willing or at least unsuspecting driver's car and coast all the way. Leland Beck, about 20 and single, lived with his grandmother. His uncles had bought him a nifty Model T Ford. A cousin of Warren's, he readily agreed to the bicycle fete. All of us excited spectators stationed ourselves strategically along the exhibition route. Warren tied the rope from the bike to the bumper. Down the hill the two of them went, the Model T cackling as it reached higher speed near the bridge, and Warren, holding tight while maintaining his stage presence. As the pace slowed near the top of the next hill, Warren simply loosened the rope, turned around and made the return trip without motorized assistance. We greeted his return as if he were a conquering hero. He conquered our fears, entertained us like a circus performer and best of all, he made us laugh.

Warren's younger brother Wallace was a close friend of Cliff. If Warren was daring in our minds, we considered Wallace to be debonaire. The youngest in his family, he received much attention and gifts from his older brothers who had left home and gone to the city to work. He was the only boy we knew who wore jodphurs and high lace-up boots. God, how we envied him. He had more marbles than anyone and he loved to play for keeps with Cliff. On his regular visits to our house Cliff usually won the lion's share of Wallace's steelies, agates and glassies. But no matter, Wallace could always get more from his brothers. Cliff and Wallace played checkers and cards, too. They shared trapping secrets and hunted rabbits and squirrels with their rifles. Theirs was a lasting friendship.

Even after Grandpa and Grandma Sevits retired from active farming they continued to maintain two workhorses, Dan and Ribbon, for the sole purpose of pulling the buggy. In the summer the horses roamed free in the large pasture area which extended down to the creek and into the woods. When we lived nearby, and certainly without Ma's knowledge, we went into the woods with an apple or hand full of sugar and started calling, "Here, Dan. Here, Ribbon." In no time at all the two docile animals came to us to receive their treat. With primitive skill we mounted their bare backs, got a firm grip on their manes and with the yell of a banshee, rode off through the woods. We didn't wish to risk being seen in the open pasture even though we knew the riding would be more pleasant there. Down the paths and into the semidry creek bed we trotted, uphill and down until both horse and rider were tired. Occasionally we were caught in the act. After a strong lecture from Grandpa on the dangers of riding between trees and under low branches, we were forgiven until the next time.

Improper handling of horses can be hazardous as Cleo and Cliff learned one lazy summer afternoon when they were trying to train a colt at the Sandry place. Ma and I had gone across the hollow to visit a family on the other side. It was Ma's intention to stay only an hour or two, so she gave her usual safety admonitions to the boys when we left. We took two-year-old Shirley with us and left Robert, four, in the boys' care. The colt was not quite a yearling, but the boys decided if they started working with him now they could count on riding him by next spring. First, they simply let him go around in a circle at the end of a lead rope. He seemed so gentle that they placed an improvised saddle pad across his back. At this he rebeled, threw up his heels and struck little Robert who fell to the ground unconscious. The boys were terrified. His lack of consciousness was only temporary and Robert was back on his feet in no time. Cleo remembered that someone who has been struck in the head should not be allowed to go to sleep. His efforts to keep little Robert from falling asleep failed. When Ma and I returned the first sight she beheld was Robert lying on the day bed with a lace curtain draped from head to toe. Ma cried out, "My God, is this baby dead?"

"No, no," Cleo replied. "He is only sleeping. We put the lace curtain over him to keep the flies away." Then he told her about the accident with the colt.

Ma pulled the curtain back and examined him carefully. He did have a nice bump on his forehead, but no apparent permanent damage. Ma said, "Thank God he wasn't hurt badly. But you boys do know he could have been, don't you? I hope you have learned that you must not work with horses when your dad isn't home."

Fun times often ended in near tragedy. When the daily newspaper started running the new comic strip, "Alley Oop," the boys thought it would be fun to mimic his prehistoric antics. One July day they were leaping from limb to limb in the big oak tree near the road, when Jimmy lost his footing and grabbed for what he thought was a sturdy branch. It was dead and brittle. When he let go of the branch behind him and grasped the brittle one, it gave way hurtling him to the earth some 12 feet below. When Dad ran to pick him up he knew that Jimmy's arm was broken. Dad shouted to Cleo, "Run up to John Byrd's and see if Roy will take us into town to the doctor."

Without a word Cleo ran as fast as his legs would go. He was back in minutes. Dad, Roy and Jimmy made the trip into town. When they got back, Jimmy, slightly pale from the ordeal, was sporting a neat white sling and a metal splint. Dad ruled the oak tree off limits for the rest of the summer.

Jimmy suffered more than his share of near tragedies. He had tagged along with the older boys, over their protests, one Sunday afternoon and had accompanied them on a swimming excursion to the Chariton River. Unable to swim, he had promised Dad he would only go in the shallow water. The older boys were to take turns watching after him. "After all," Dad reasoned, "the boy has to learn to swim some time." Besides, some of the men would be swimming there, too. Because she didn't swim, and therefore had a great fear of the water, Ma protested even more than the boys. She didn't think Jimmy should go.

The afternoon progressed without incident, the men and boys splashing, diving and swimming. Suddenly, quite a distance from the others, Jimmy was shouting, "Help!" Under the surface he slipped, bobbed up and again shouted, "Help!" By the time the men reached him he was going down for the third time.

When he was safely out of the water, he was blue from lack of oxygen and shivering from fear. One of the men quickly wrapped a towel around him and rubbed him dry. After he was dressed, Uncle Jake drove him home, grumbling all the way. He contended that all the boys needed a good licking. They had disobeyed. When they got home Ma was momentarily inclined to agree with Jake, but because she was thankful the boys were all safe, she said firmly, "If you men were there and knew he couldn't swim, you should have assumed the responsibility. We are lucky he is alive."

No matter what instructions Ma or Dad gave us, particularly in matters of our safety, it seemed we often did just the opposite. One early spring day I begged Ma to let me go to visit my friend, Helen. It was too soon to go barefoot, so Ma agreed to let me go, on the condition that I would promise not to remove my shoes. I promised. I had no more than arrived at Helen's home, about a mile and a half away, when we took off our shoes to jump off the chicken roost barefoot into a pile of straw. Oh it was great fun! Repeatedly we climbed to the top of the pole roost and leaped into the straw pile below.

On my last jump something awful happened. Somewhere in the midst of that pile of straw was a short board with a long nail, sharp end up. When I landed on it, the nail pierced my foot and came through at the top. The pain and fear of the injury were not uppermost in my mind. I had betrayed a promise to Ma. How could I face her? Helen and her mother held the board down and firmly removed my foot from the nail. After soaking the wound with turpentine, Helen's mother wrapped my foot with clean muslin.

To insure my safe return home, Helen walked with me. I was glad I didn't have to face Ma alone. Whatever I feared from my broken promise did not materialize. Ma's concern over my injury outweighed her disappointment in my promise not kept.

The absence of commercially made toys in our home only enhanced our ability to improvise. Milton loved all things mechanical with his delight being the working part of an old alarm clock. Once when he and I had gone on an errand to Sherd and Cindy's that called for an excursion into their attic, he spotted two Big Bens. He wanted them so desperately but he could not summon up the courage to ask the elderly couple for them. Big Ben was the Cadillac of alarm clocks. The bell rang with two levels—one ear-piercing and the other subdued. With control devices for every function, it was somewhat sophisticated in a mechanical sense.

We took the bundle Ma had sent us for and started home. All the way Milton kept repeating, "I know they would give me the clocks if I only asked. They don't work or they wouldn't be in the attic. I want to go back and ask Cindy for them."

"But, Milt, " I protested, "we're half way home. Besides it's hot and I'm tired."

"Please, come back with me," he begged.

"Oh, all right. But don't blame me if you get into trouble with Ma over this," I countered.

The next question was, "How do we approach Sherd and Cindy?" It simply was not polite to beg people for anything, especially if they were older people. We had been taught forever that children respect their elders.

We thought and thought, and finally Milton exclaimed, "I have it! I know what I'll do."

"O.K. what are you going to do." I demanded.

"Well, I'm going to say: 'Sherd, I think I can fix those two Big Bens in your attic. Will you give me a chance to try?' That's how I'm going to do it, " he explained.

As we walked back up the hill nearing Sherd and Cindy's back door, Milton kept rehearsing what he would say. When we arrived, he delivered his lines with the skill of a professional actor. At first Sherd and Cindy could not recall having the alarm clocks.

Milt said, "Come with me; I'll show them to you."

Dutifully Sherd and Cindy followed up the stairs while Milt ran ahead to point to the clocks. "See, these are the ones I mean," said Milton as he gestured toward the clocks.

"Oh, those clocks," acknowledged Sherd. "They have been out of order for years. You could never make them work."

"Please, just let me try," pleaded Milton.

"All right, boy. Take them with you. You can have them to keep for yourself," Sherd replied.

Those two clocks kept Milton occupied for weeks as he contemplated the workings of all the intricate gadgetry unique to the Big Ben.

After careful oiling and readjusting of screws and springs, both clocks ran like new again. Milton, so pleased with his accomplishment, made a special trip to Sherd and Cindy's to show them what he had been able to do with the clocks. He kept one to tinker with for himself, but the better of the two he presented to Ma.

We always attributed Milton's uncanny mechanical ability to the fact that he was left-handed. By the same token we felt Robert's artistic talent was due to his left-handedness.

There was no doubt, Robert showed artistic ability at an early age.

When he was only four years old and with no picture books for models, using a two-for-a-penny lead pencil, he drew a complicated farm scene on the side of the corrugated cardboard carton we used for a wood box behind the kitchen stove. As we all gathered around in amazement at his creative genius, we asked questions.

"What are those little round things here?"

"Oh, they're Tanry's apples," he answered.

"And what do we have here?" asked Dad.

"Well, here is the barn and in this little stall is our pig," Robert explained. He had been careful to leave no details to the imagination. As he progressed through grade school, his art work helped him to become the pride of the teacher and his brothers and sisters. Ma and Dad were proud, too.

As a little girl I often longed for a beautiful baby doll. I had seen pictures of dolls dressed in long white dresses and crisp bonnets in the mail-order catalog. My Uncle Forest who lived in Waterloo, Iowa, had a niece who occasionally sent outgrown clothes to me. One Christmas she sent a big baby doll. Oh, I loved that dolly. When spring came I took her to school to play with at recess. My first-grade classmate, Bennie Dolan, and I played in our improvised playhouse made simply from branches laid down to form the outline of rooms. Some of the older girls brought canning jar lids and broken pieces of china for dishes. We took turns holding my big baby doll. When the teacher rang the handbell signaling the end of recess, we dropped everything and ran inside. One day I forgot and left my baby doll out overnight. An overnight shower wreaked havoc on my beautiful doll. I was horrified when I discovered what the rain had done to her composition face. It had become a grotesque glob and her cotton-stuffed body was all wet and soggy. I think I felt the same grief a real mother felt with the loss of a real baby.

Cleo possessed uncanny ability to create playthings for us from rather unconventional materials. For me he made dollhouse furniture from scraps of wood. He sewed cuddly stuffed cats, monkeys and bears from old socks or leg sections of worn-out long underwear, or pieces of fabric cut from old denim overalls, wool coats or sweaters. He gave them button eyes and embroidered mouths and noses.

Cleo made little rubber-band propelled wooden tractors. On either end of a large empty wooden thread spool he cut notches for traction. Then he made a rubber band by tying the ends of a strip of rubber cut from an old inner tube. Next, he broke a matchstick for one end just the same length as the diameter of the spool, and inserted it through the rubber band. At the other end he used a full-length matchstick inserted through the rubber band. Then he added a little rub of a bar of soap to lubricate for easy winding. Now simply wind up the rubber band with the long stick and the race can begin. We entertained ourselves for hours with the boys' tractor competition.

An outdoor toy we all loved was the hoop and paddle. Many hardware items, particularly nails, came in wooden kegs, with one of two small iron hoops at either end and a larger one in the middle. Grandpa Sevits' machine shed housed plenty of wooden kegs with iron hoops. Cleo made us each a paddle which resembled a "T". An old plaster lath was just right for the standard hoop paddle. Cleo adjusted the length of the paddle to the height of the user. Then he attached a short piece about six inches long across the bottom to form the paddle for the hoop. The object of the hoop and paddle was to keep the hoop under control, yet always rolling. It took great patience and much practice to perfect the art.

Glen and Hop Stafford, perhaps Cleo and Cliff's best friends, were members of a large family headed by a widowed mother. They were just as poor as we were, causing us to share a common bond. Cleo loved music and wanted to learn to play the fiddle. Glen played the fiddle and Hop played the guitar. No matter how diligently Cleo listened and watched he was never able to master the fiddle. Often when the music lessons lasted longer than Dad considered necessary, he'd ask the boys to leave. They never seemed to be offended and came back often.

Cleo finally decided that if he couldn't learn to play the fiddle he would satisfy his love for music with a phonograph. The Stafford boys had an old Edison cylinder model they had taken as payment for work they did for a widow lady. It was great, but the music was limited to the cylinders which came with it. No replacements were available. Cleo wanted a modern phonograph with regular disk records so he could buy or trade for his own. Glen and Hop knew an old lady who lived near their sister over by Connelsville who had a fine hand-cranked disk-playing phonograph. Because the boys' older sister was a good friend of Ma's, she volunteered to borrow Grandpa and Grandma Sevits' team and buggy to drive over to see Mona and to get the phonograph. The trip was an all day excursion.

Ma, Cleo and the baby were exhausted when they returned home. But we all stood close by while Cleo wound up the motor with the hand crank, placed a record on the turntable and out came beautiful music! "On the Isle of Capri," "I Come to the Garden Alone," and "Old Rugged Cross," were all sung by great voices we had never heard before.

The central requirement for good times was simply an occasion for people to get together. Even group work projects became pleasant times with everyone sharing the work and fellowship. Butchering provided such an occasion.

It was a special day which we awaited with an expectancy and excitement comparable only to the Fourth of July or Christmas. It came early in the winter with no fixed date.

The criteria were simple: First, several days of below freezing weather must have passed; second, there must be in readiness a fine barrow around seven months old weighing about 250 pounds; finally and just as important, there must be available good neighbors. All these were necessary for a day almost as important as a national holiday—Butchering Day.

Preparation for the long-awaited event began several days earlier. If a tree with a strong branch at the correct height was available, the

Uncle Harve Sevits and Dad flanking a fat hog on butchering day

men would rig up a block and tackle to hoist the animal to the right working level. Otherwise, they busied themselves building a hoist which looked to a child like a great place to put a swing. It was quite simply two posts, probably eight feet high with a strong cross post at the top. A winch and pulley would be needed when the time came. Other essential items included a 50-gallon oil drum and a huge iron kettle, in which to heat water.

In the house the women were assembling sharp knives, pans, large skillets, canning jars and sausage grinders. They cleaned the smoke-house, making certain that all the meat hooks used the winter before had been carefully preserved for this butchering day. They reviewed their recipes for sausage and for ham curing.

On the final evening just prior to butchering day, the specially fed and nurtured porker was carefully separated from the rest of the herd and kept overnight in his own little house.

At last, the big day is here. Neighbors arrive early, ready to take on the challenge of the day. The children are given breakfast and hurried off to school.

First the men build a fire beneath the big iron kettle, then carry water from the well to fill it almost to the brim. When they are convinced the fire is full-blown and the water will be hot when needed, they proceed to the most unpleasant task of the day. They approach the hog lot with somber faces. One man is armed with a .22 caliber rifle and the other with a pointed, razor-sharp knife. They open the sliding door on the isolation quarters and the beautiful animal bolts out to greet the morning. Quickly, the man with the gun takes careful aim and the bullet pierces the skull just between the eyes. Swiftly, the man with the knife slips the sharp point into the jugular vein and waits for the blood to leave the flinching body. The grim task is finished.

Now the work begins. The men each grab a hind leg and drag the animal to the hoist. They attach the winch and pulley to the hind legs and raise the animal into the air. The oil drum is placed directly below the hog and quickly filled with boiling water from the kettle. The carcass is lowered again and again into the boiling water to soften and loosen the bristles which abound on a hog's body. When the men are certain the softening and loosening process is complete, they hoist the carcass up and start scraping the skin to remove the bristles. Then they splash him with buckets of water to wash away the hair.

The next step requires precision and skill. The animal must be eviscerated, but not carelessly. Some of the internal organs, such as the heart and liver are edible. Further, the fat found around the kidneys produces the highest quality lard—leaf lard. And, of course, the intestines must be emptied with great care so they can be washed and used for sausage stuffing.

An expert with hands as deft as a surgeon's, is given the job of evisceration. A slip of the knife could spill the gall bladder, or puncture the stomach, causing damage to the rest of the carcass. Following this unpleasant task, the men again douse the carcass with several buckets of cold water, leave it to hang for a while to chill thoroughly, and take a much-deserved break, joining the women in the kitchen for coffee, or even breakfast if they started their work before eating.

With the break ended, the women prepare the kitchen for their part of the processing and the men return to the butchering. They lower the carcass and place it on a specially constructed outdoor table. First, they remove the hams, shoulders, head, tail and feet. Then they cut a roast or two and remove the tenderloin for the special treat of the day. Most of the rest of the meat is removed from the bone to be ground and made into sausage.

As quickly as possible the women start grinding. When they have enough ground pork for a batch of sausage, they add the salt, pepper, and rubbed sage. They fry some of the sausage in patties and place it in canning jars, pour hot grease over the patties and seal the jars. Some of the ground meat they stuff into the cleaned intestines, for use in the next few weeks or for smoking in the smokehouse with the hams and bacon.

When the men have deboned all the meat and prepared the sides for bacon, they clean up and begin preparing the hams and shoulders for curing. Several methods were in use then for curing meat. One was to inject a strong salt brine into the artery of the ham with a large hypodermic syringe. Another was to soak the meat for a few days in a salt brine. Still another was simply to coat and rub the exterior of the meat with a curing mixture. But, whichever method was used, it was followed with a smoking process, using specially selected hickory wood for the fire.

Naturally, since the aging and curing process took some time, farm families depended on the fresh meat first and the cured meat later. Two of the most delicious butchering day pork dishes were the delicately flavored tenderloin, fried or roasted, and the succulent fresh ham steaks or fresh ham roast. One or the other was reserved for the evening meal when the school children could join in the joy of the delicious treat.

Children were generally excluded from the actual butchering process due to the hazards of boiling water, hot grease and sharp knives. However, children joined in the fun of roasted pig tail and ears or munching cracklin's left over from lard making. No one who grew up in the 1930s is likely to forget the excitement of butchering day.

Chapter Nine

Dear Hearts and Gentle People

So many special people made us feel good about ourselves and gave meaning to our lives. At the top of the list were our dear grandparents, Grandpa and Grandma Sevits and Grandma May. We never knew our Grandpa May. He died before we were born.

A child's blessings can be measured by his access to his grandparents. We were blessed because we lived within walking distance of Grandma and Grandpa Sevits most of the time, and near our Grandma May when we lived away from them.

Grandma Sevits was born in a German colony called Bethel and later came to Nineveh Colony, which eventually became the town of Connelsville. She and Grandpa were both of German descent. Their badge of honor was hard work coupled with honesty. Grandma's favorite compliment to pay a young person was, "You're a good little worker." They both worked hard from the predawn hours until after sunset. They went to bed early and got up early. Their 80-acre farm had been a dowry from her father, Peter Voelker, later changed to Felker. Grandpa Sevits worked in the coal mines when he was younger to supplement the farm income to raise their family of 12 children.

Although Grandma had worked hard all her life she was endowed with grace and a kind of regal beauty. Pictures of her as a girl confirmed that she was truly a lovely young woman. Soft curls framed her forehead and dark eyes. She stood tall and erect, graceful yet confident. She had a firm business head and was the decision maker. Grandpa was more inclined to let someone take advantage of him in a business deal.

I can still remember clearly every detail of their little farmstead. The huge full-length-of-the-house kitchen across the south side provided the focal point for most of the activity. Two windows on the south and one on the west gave access to the winter sun for Grandma's indoor garden of beautiful blooming plants. Her Christmas

Mary Elizabeth Felker and William Emerson Sevits official wedding picture September 11, 1888

cactus cascaded down the sides of the big blue speckled kettle-planter in potato-peeling-like streams interrupted with a pink blossom every three or four inches. Because her geraniums bloomed all year long, she always brought flowers to church for the altar or for funerals. In addition, there were magnificent oleanders standing tall, sporting clusters of pink blossoms, amarylisses, giant bright crimson, salmon and white, angel wing begonias with their huge wing-like leaves, and stately ferns. She gave them tender loving care throughout the winter in the house and as soon as it was safe to move them outdoors, she transferred the blooming garden to a safe, sheltered spot where the exposure to the sun would be just right.

Her kitchen began with the big wood-burning cookstove. Grandma's stove featured a large capacity reservoir, something our stove never had. It supplied a constant supply of hot water. Displayed on all the walls surrounding the big kitchen stove hung all the kitchen gadgets one could imagine—wooden spoons, meat forks, knives of varying size, slicers, graters, corkscrews, spatulas, wood cutting boards, stove accessories, skillets, pans, cookie cutters—any and every thing needed for food preparation. To the right of the stove stood a low work table with a storage shelf below. Because of the proximity to the reservoir, the table provided a good place to wash dishes or prepare food. The water pail, along with canisters of various staples, was arranged at the back for easy access. To the right of this table an oak cabinet rose almost to the ceiling. Oddly enough very little kitchen work was ever done on this cabinet; it really served more as a bookkeeping center.

In the southwest corner a little black cupboard which housed the everyday dishes, salt and pepper, spices, leftovers for the next meal, the sugar bowl and spoon holder, stood about five feet high. The two top drawers above the dish storage area contained a variety of gadgets Grandma had saved for playthings for little visitors. That cupboard emitted an aroma of spice, jelly and other good things such as no candy store could duplicate.

Between the display of blooming plants in the west window and the big dining table was the one mechanical marvel in Grandma's kitchen, the DeLaval cream separator.

Dominating the otherwise humble scene a tall glass-doored safe proudly displayed gold trimmed china, cut glassware and family heirlooms. Grandma saved these dishes for special occasions.

Next, came the huge dining table which in the past had seated the whole family. Now Grandma and Grandpa sat at right angles from each other at the southeast end of the table. A long bench extended from one end of the table to the other on the back side, providing adequate seating space for several uncles and aunts when there was a family get-together. Grandpa drank coffee from a mustache cup, while Grandma sipped hot water with cream added.

At 4:30 in the morning, while it was yet dark, Grandpa called softly, "Time to get up." Oh, how you would love to remain in bed, but the motivation for jumping out quickly was quite simply, breakfast. Grandma served a breakfast fit for the emperor of some far off land. First, she fried delicious home-cured ham, and in the same fryings, eggs for those who wanted them. Next came the milk gravy. She always made a big skillet full so there would be plenty for the cats to enjoy their morning treat. On the side she heated a bit of hominy or sauerkraut. On the table were two or three kinds of jelly, sorghum molasses and honey. A little tin can with a wire bail at the top contained the remains of the cream which trickled out of the cream separator the evening before at the end of the cream separating process. Hot biscuits rounded out the meal. But the special treat we got only at Grandma's was Post Toasties. Served as a kind of dessert to top off the huge meal in little gold trimmed sauce dishes, the Post Toasties were generously sprinkled with sugar and drenched in the cream tricklings. Corn flakes would never taste that good in a lifetime.

It was not possible to leave Grandma's kitchen hungry. She loved to cook and entertain. Her favorite occasion for a dinner was to invite all the church family down for an outdoor dinner after church. A natural grove of trees in the southwest corner of the big yard provided the just-right shelter for an outdoor dinner. Rustic board tables seemed to a child to be at least a mile long. Although it was her regular custom to bake every Saturday, when she was planning to serve the church dinner, she baked for several days. There were pies of apple and pumpkin, custard and mincemeat and sometimes coconut cream or lemon meringue. There were spice cakes, hickory nut cakes and apple dumplings. Fried chicken, stewed chicken with noodles, sausage, ham, sauerkraut, hominy, breaded tomatoes, green beans, corn, fresh radishes, green onions and wilted lettuce all from the garden, and all kinds of pickles and relishes rounded out the menu.

The men ate heartily and in the afternoon Grandpa led them in several rounds of horseshoe. The children ran to the car shed to play in the old Model T or chased each other over the cellar or ran and played hide and seek in the orchard.

The women washed the dishes, exchanged recipes and gossip. Too soon the afternoon ended and each family departed as they had arrived, in cars, on foot or in buggies. Many would scarcely have

*Grandpa and Grandma
Sevits, the hosts*

*Friends, cousins, aunts and uncles
enjoying a Sunday at Grandma Sevits*

One of Grandma Sevits' famous mile-long outdoor dinners

time to complete their evening chores before returning to the church for prayer service.

In the winter when we all got together at Grandma's at Thanksgiving or Christmas, we dispersed all over the house. Our favorite place to explore was "the room." Probably a parlor by description, Grandma simply called it "the room." First of all, a gorgeous ornate high wood-framed bed commanded the center of attention in the room. A matching dresser and occasional table boasted white marble tops.

In comfortable seating arrangment stood three beautiful rocking chairs all equipped with satin or velvet cushions. On the wall just above the dresser hung a majestic buck deer's head.

My favorite spot in the whole room was Grandpa's writing desk. A row of law books, in which Grandpa was well read, lined the shelf at the top. And above that hung the lithograph, "Battle of Shiloh." The soldiers fell from their horses, charged with their bayonets, carried the flag and blew the bugle all in precise detail. The scene, though frightening, made the Civil War come alive for me.

We derived great pleasure from playing Grandma's foot-pumped reed organ. With a little practice one could learn a few harmonious chords. Occasionally Ma played while we sang. The organ also served as a place to display all the latest family portraits.

But the portrait of our Uncle Sherman who had served in France in World War I occupied the most prominent place in the room. Situated above the headboard of the big bed, framed in gold and tinted with natural colors, his picture was larger than life.

Because the floor was covered with an elegant red and gold Persian rug, the room felt warm even though it was not heated.

The only way to gain access to the room was to pass through the front room. The hub of activity for Grandpa and Grandma's cozy house, it also provided access to the upstairs. The slightly diminutive pot-bellied stove radiated warmth in the winter and, of course, with the stairway door left open, warmed the bedrooms upstairs, too. Grandpa and Grandma slept on a leather-upholstered, horse-hair-filled duofold, a combination bed by night and comfortable couch during the day. Grandma kept her mending in the under-stairway storage area in a neat little wood chest. When the door was open we could play hide and seek and climb through the little triangle created by the open door away from the stairs.

At the window just between the stairway storage and the duofold stood a stately tall narrow table topped with a magnificent Boston fern. Just as the three bears each had their own chair, so did Grandma and Grandpa. But they also had extra chairs for company.

The coziness of the front room was not its special feature. We looked upon the hand-cranked, battery-powered wall telephone as a magic box. To reach the operator in Greentop, one simply turned the crank several times creating a "long." We recognized Grandma's ring as two "longs" and a "short." When Grandma and Grandpa were out doing the chores, we listened in on other conversations. Grandma would never permit it when she was in the house, so we always bore a burden of guilt when they came back from the barn. We soon discovered as the receivers clicked down the line we weren't the only ones listening. Sometimes one of the listeners chimed in to ask or answer a question.

The most exciting addition to the front room, a gift from all the family, was the multi-band, battery-powered, push-button radio. On a clear night we heard the announcer say, "This is Radio Station WHO in Des Moines," or "KMOX in St. Louis," or "WGN in Chicago," or "KFEQ in St. Joseph." KFEQ and WHO gave lots of hog markets and farm reports. But the latest popular songs came in on WGN and KMOX, as did popular artists such as Fred Allen and Jack Benny.

Given Grandma's austere, German background, she considered the radio a frivolous luxury. But her eyes softened and her feet shuffled when she recognized the music of a schottische. It was then my schoolgirl curiosity prompted me to ask, "Tell me what it was like when you were a girl, please Grandma." How I loved to hear her tell the story.

"The ladies all lined up on one side of the room and the men on the other. Then after a bow from the gentleman and a curtsy from his partner, we danced the evening away. Come over here Will and let's show her how we did it." After a little coaxing and in the somewhat limited space of the front room, Grandpa joined Grandma to give me a rare performance of the neat little German folk dance, the schottische.

Grandpa loved the news and farm reports. But his greatest delight came from election hoopla. Learned in the law, a justice of the peace and a notary public, he was sometimes a candidate for office. Politics at the national, state and local levels fed his soul. To go to Kirksville and sit on the benches at the courthouse and talk politics with his cronies gave him unlimited satisfaction.

One of the greatest pleasures I remember sharing with Grandpa was to help him hitch up the horses and buggy to make the weekly trip to the general store. Grandma had already filled the egg cases to capacity and prepared the cream in its special can. She made out her shopping list making sure to include a bag of candy.

Grandpa kept the buggy in a little two-compartment shed just west of the house. Called the car shed, it probably got its name from the fact that a long since nonfunctioning Model T Ford touring car sat majestically in the other compartment.

The old car remained in the car shed as the last remnant of memorabilia from their youngest son, Hershel. He had been gone from home several years and the car wasn't working when he left, but Grandma wouldn't allow it to be moved. Grandchildren were permitted to "drive" the Model T all we wanted. We could make "pretend" trips to North Dakota, Iowa and Nebraska, just as our aunts and uncles had done in the "old days."

We were not permitted to play in the buggy. Because the buggy was their only form of transportation besides walking, we treated it with respect. The top was covered with rubber-coated cloth and there were windows at the sides and back. Upholstered with black leather, the seats provided a comfortable ride. The high dashboard gave protection from splashing mud and from the horses' natural requirements.

Oh, it was great fun to ride along on a bright morning and greet all the neighbors as we clippity-clopped on our way to the store. And when we arrived there, we would meet still others who were doing their weekly trading as well. We found out all the news, good and bad, about friends and neighbors whom we had not seen since the last visit to the store. The men talked of politics, hog prices and the weather. Women talked of gardens, babies, sewing and church goings-on. We always left reluctantly, as did the other traders, for we as they had chores to do and so our trading ended before we were ready to terminate the weekly visit. Grandma would be anxious about us and would be worried if we were late for our noon meal.

As soon as we got back home our first order of business was to tell Grandma all the news. After a tasty hot lunch Grandma shared a bit of the special candy treat brought from the store.

The aura of Grandma and Grandpa's place extended beyond the house. The neatly kept yard surrounded by a slightly dilapidated

fence with front and back gates, abounded with a variety of flowers
scheduled to bloom the entire warm season of the year. First came
the lilacs' delicate fragrance. Then the white mock orange and pink
almond blossom, followed in immediate succession by the red,
yellow and white roses. Blue wisteria and fragrant honeysuckle
drooped down in clusters from the sagging arbor built purposely to
display their beauty. Orange and brown bugle flowers that crept
along the fence made a haven for the humming birds.

Bounding the yard on the north and serving as protection from the
north winter wind and the dust and noise of the road, were stately tall
ancient cedar evergreen trees standing like soldiers at parade rest.
Robins, cardinals and blue jays flitting through the branches created
beautiful nature pictures in the early morning sunlight.

Just to the east of the back porch stood the multipurpose smokehouse. Because its concrete floor made penetration by vermin virtually impossible, products requiring protection from such infestation
were stored there. Bran "shorts," a hog feed supplement, was kept in
the smokehouse to be added to whey or sour milk at feeding time.
Extra egg cases, milk and cream cans and other milking parapherna-
lia were also stored in the smokehouse.

Looking somewhat like a miniature underground home with a
conventionally roofed and sided entry way was the symbol of survival,
the fruit cellar. Located just south of the smokehouse it provided
storage space for canned fruits and vegetables and a cooling place
for cream, milk and butter, eggs and other perishables. In a high
windstorm, Grandma and Grandpa retreated to the cellar for shelter.

Hollyhocks of every color danced around the cellar mound and
even skipped past the south fence into the orchard. The orchard
boasted practically every kind of fruit-bearing tree indigenous to
northeast Missouri. There were little white-meated cling peaches
and large luscious Elbertas. Red cherries, plums, Bartlett pears and a
variety of apples from Delicious to Jonathan to Grimes Golden could
be found there. On the other side of the garden the late August air
would be laden with the pungent aroma of large purple Concord
grapes. Within the confines of Grandma's kitchen garden, in addition to all kinds of vegetables were her well-tended raspberries,
blackberries and strawberries.

The neatly fenced yard provided a calm, peaceful and beautiful
setting. But the primary purpose of the fence was to keep the
chickens confined to their proper domain, the area outside. Just on

the other side of the fence which bounded the east, were Grandma's henhouses and chicken coops. Situated a proper distance from the house, the outdoor toilet was also fenced outside the yard.

Grandma treated all the farm animals in her care with kindness. In the winter months she heated the drinking water for the chickens and cooked vegetable peelings to feed with their corn and oats to add a little warmth. Some people thought she was too kind to her cats. Every morning she prepared a large skillet of milk gravy, and after removing what she and Grandpa needed for breakfast, she filled the skillet with milk and set it out for the cats. She and Grandpa shared the philosophy of kindness to animals. Workhorses were never overworked or mistreated. Their dogs, Buster and Lad, got their regular baths every week.

Grandpa's tool shed which stood just to the north of the back gate on the other side of the wood pile, housed every kind of tool imaginable. There were shovels, hoes, scythes, sickles, saws, hammers, planes and axes. The aroma of lubricating oil permeated the shed. A giant anvil dominated the center of attention. On a brisk fall day we often circled around the anvil to crack hickory nuts, eating every other one and yet hoping to accumulate enough for a hickory nut cake. A crib for storage of unshelled corn joined the tool shed.

Some of the most delightful memories of Grandma and Grandpa's place are associated with their little barn. Originally built for living quarters, it had been converted to a barn when their new home was built. The hayloft could be reached with regular stairs instead of a conventional ladder. Bolted to the floor close to the grain bins was Grandma's chicken feed grinder. The distant clankety-clank of the feed grinder gave a clear signal that Grandma and Grandpa were doing the chores in the barn, even from quite a distance down the road. We liked to turn the crank on the big red grinder and watch the chopped chicken feed come out of the spout.

While Grandma ground chicken feed, Grandpa herded the milk cows into their stalls. In the winter they were kept in the barn lot. But in summer they were turned out into the pasture for grazing. We were allowed to watch Grandma and Grandpa milking their favorite cows only if we kept quiet and stayed out of the way. As we grew older we were permitted to milk the gentler cows under close supervision.

Bringing the cows in from the pasture in the summer was one of my favorite chores at Grandma's. A long lane skirted the corn and

*Grandma Sevits and Cousin Icel cuddling
the adorable puppies*

oats fields and led to the pasture, the water hole in the branch, and the shade trees in the big woods. There is no sound as sweet as the tinkle of cow bells and the occasional moo as the cows move placidly homeward in the evening. It really wasn't necessary to go and bring them in. They came of their own volition. However, they chose their own time to do so. We went to get them because Grandma preferred to milk them at her convenience, not theirs.

In addition to the garden near the house, Grandma and Grandpa maintained at least two truck patches for as long as I can remember, or at least as long as their health remained good. Every day they picked up hoes and whatever additional equipment they needed, Grandpa with his sweat-stained straw hat and Grandma wearing a slat bonnet on her head and stocking legs on her arms to protect her from the sun. They trudged religiously to the truck patches to cultivate the earth and remove the weeds. With their big family grown and gone, they no longer needed all the produce. So, when we lived nearby we benefited from the surplus.

I could continue to describe the place where Grandma and Grandpa lived. I could tell about the sheep pasture just north of the road, and the berry patch in the upper hillside cow pasture where blackberries grew wild, or the huge hickory tree just west of the house on the way to the mailbox. But the memories of Grandma and Grandpa were more than just of a place. The memories were of special friends. Yes, that's it. They were friends. They were not indulging pals. But instead, they were stern, strict, loving, caring friends. They took time to teach such things as how to disassemble and reassemble the cream separator—or how to hitch the harness for the buggy—or just the right mix for chicken feed—or how to adjust the yoke to fit more comfortably when carrying water from the pond—or just the right measurements of salt for making sauerkraut. Through their patience, I learned a number of survival skills. Through their example I learned that honesty and kindness to others were primary in the pursuit of happiness. Their life was simple. But the gratification I derived from that simplicity has sustained me through the years.

Grandma May was quite different from Grandma Sevits, but special in her own way. She had endured an extremely difficult childhood. She had been raised by foster parents who had not treated her kindly. She married at 15, had a family of 15 children, three of whom died in infancy, and was left a widow shortly after the birth of her youngest. Because widows in those days were vulnerable to the whims of traveling peddlers and neighboring rogues, Grandma May put on a rather tough exterior. She carried a pistol and rode a horse—not side-saddle as proper ladies should—but stride-saddle, just like men. She traded her oats and corn and sold hogs and cattle in the same market place as men. Her children, boys and girls alike, had to work hard to make the poor soil of her Putnam County hills produce enough food for a living.

Joseph Sylvester May and Margaret Elizabeth Stokesberry in the early years of their marriage. He died in 1916.

Grandma's little house stood proudly at the top of one of those wooded hills. The entire family had grown up here in the two-room cottage with additional sleeping space in the loft.

As if the hardships Grandma May had endured were not enough, in the mid 1930s she began to lose her sight and was totally blind in a few short years. Life would have been bleak indeed except that her youngest son Harvey who had stayed on the farm with her, married and moved his bride into the tiny cottage. As the young couple began to have their family, Grandma was not a burden. She continued to cook and help with housework and child care. She made the greatest biscuits ever. She didn't roll them on a floured board in the conventional way. She simply pinched off the right amount of dough, formed it into an oval and arranged it in the pan so as not to touch the other biscuits, thus allowing a crisp crust to form all around.

While the biscuits baked, Grandma May fried thick slices of bacon just until they were well done, not crisp. After the bacon was removed from the pan, she added milk to the hot grease which created sop to dip biscuits in. For anyone who didn't care for sop, there was a selection of honey from Uncle Harvey's bee hives, Grandma's homemade crab apple jelly or sorghum molasses.

A tiny woman with silver gray hair pulled back tightly into a bun in the back, Grandma May wore a floor-length cotton dress protected by an apron gathered and tied at the waist. She smoked strong tobacco in a clay pipe. Although not formally educated, she possessed a sharp wit and an uncanny ability for storytelling, particularly ghost stories. On a cold winter night with a wood fire burning brightly we often urged her to tell us one of her favorites.

"Now, young'ns, gather 'round and I'll try and remember the time I ran into the devil in the graveyard," she'd announce invitingly. Immediately a hush fell over her little house and our eyes glowed with anticipation.

"Well, it was dark as pitch that moonless night," she began. "I had walked over to the Low Ground store early in the afternoon to get a poke of sugar when one of the Parton boys came running in and asked if I would come with him to be with his wife while he went to fetch the doctor. I really needed to get back home, but he seemed desperate, so I went with him. Her baby wasn't due for another couple of weeks, but no matter, that baby had decided to make an early appearance. What seemed like an eternity passed, and poor Mizz Parton knew that baby wasn't gonna wait 'till the doctor got there. She asked me, 'Mrs. May, have you ever delivered a baby?' 'Well, I've catched a many a one,' I told her. So, together Mizz Parton and me brought that fine baby boy into the world.

It was dark when her man got back with the doctor so I picked up my poke of sugar and started walking home.

As you know, the Cain-Ford Cemetery is just on the other side of Low Ground, and Blackbird Creek is at the bottom of the hill. As I passed through the graveyard and neared the creek, there before my very eyes rose a giant fiery demon. 'My God,' I cried. 'Are you the devil?' Not a word came in reply. 'Well, who are you?' I demanded. Still no answer.

It had been a long day and I was tired. Maybe this was all in my imagination. But then the form lunged forward and gave out a strange grunt. The grunt had a familiar ring, but I couldn't be sure.

I had no choice; I had to find out who or what the fiery form was and what it was doing in the graveyard. I summoned up all the courage within my soul and moved closer and closer until the grunt became an oink. Now I knew! The spooky, fiery figure moving close to the earth was no longa a mystery. It was Bub Sol's old sow that had got out of the pen and rooted in the foxfire in the swamp. So you see, tadpoles, no matter how afeared you are of something, the more you learn about it, the less it frightens you. So, learn all you can about whatever it is you are afeared of and you'll find it won't scare you as much in the light of understanding."

Another favorite was the story of how she ran the pushy peddler off her property.

"Well, one hot summer day I was a-washin' my clothes in the wash-tub out in the back yard, when this slick city dude pulled up to the fence and come bouncin' into the yard with his satchel full of ribbons and lace. 'Good morning, little lady,' said he. 'Mornin' said I. 'I think I can add a little spice to your life with my ribbons and lace; would you like to see my wares?' he asked. There was something about the man I didn't trust, but maybe I was being unfair. So, I said, 'I'm busy washing clothes but I'll take a quick look.'

He started to take his satchel toward the door, but I said, 'No, I'll look at your wares here in the yard, if you don't mind.'

'O.K.' says he, 'but they would look much nicer spread out on your bed.' With that he moved closer and slipped his arm around my waist. Quickly I moved over near the boiling wash pot, dipped up a pitcher of hot lye water and looking him right in the eye, I said, 'Mister, unless you get out of my yard and off my property this minute I'll douse you with this boiling lye water until your eyes look like bullets.' He left in a cloud of dust, the likes of which you've never seen. Heh! Heh! I think he knew I'd do it, too."

Next to our grandparents Beulah and Gene were our best loved relatives. Because the couple was childless and because Ma and Beulah were twin sisters, we benefited from a very close relationship. Gene worked in the coal mine when they lived in Novinger and later in a farm machinery factory in Waterloo, Iowa. We thought they were well-to-do simply because they had a job, ate better food and wore better clothes than we.

When we had a new baby or when there was illness in the family, we could always count on Beulah to come and stay with us. Oh, we enjoyed her visits. She loved to cook and usually tried to make

Dad and Gene goin' fishin' in the Model "T"

Dad and Ma and their closest friends, Beulah and Gene

something special for us even from our limited food supply. When she came to stay with us when Teddy was born, finding victuals was a problem. She decided to make potato soup. There were fewer potatoes than needed so she added more water. We all laughed when four-year-old Robert cried aloud, "Look, Ma, I found a potato!"

On Christmas, birthdays and special school occasions, we knew Beulah and Gene would send us something new to wear. Patent leather shoes, a red sweater, a white shirt and tie—these were all typical of their thoughtfulness.

Gene loved to tell jokes and entertain. We loved his little hand-carved wood dancing man. The dancing man's arms and legs were jointed so that when Gene held him extended on a stick and vibrated a thin board under his feet he danced with great rhythm—clickety, clickety, clack.

The most exciting pleasure we got from Beulah and Gene was a ride in their Model T Ford touring car. And when we weren't privileged to ride in it we were equally excited to hear of their travels. We loved to hear the story of their trip to South Dakota in mid-March in a snowstorm. They left Kirksville with their nephew, Wallace Sevits. In Waterloo, Iowa, they were to pick up Beulah's brother Harvey with their ultimate destination her sister Opal's homestead in eastern South Dakota. The snowstorm started in Waterloo. Harvey's original plan was to drive his one-passenger Triumph racer and follow along behind them. However, a short distance out of Waterloo they abandoned the racer and never picked it up again.

When they reached Madison, South Dakota, they had already been on the road about 14 hours. They needed to stop and rest. It was Saturday night and they found lodging in a small hotel. The proprietors took their money in advance and asked not to be awakened on Sunday morning when they left. As they were loading up the Model T for their departure, a group of grizzly looking men asked about lodging. Gene explained that they were leaving and that the proprietors did not wish to be disturbed and invited the men to take their beds. Gene and the others laughed as they continued on their trip wondering what the hotel owners thought when they found a new set of guests in the beds previously occupied by Gene and Beulah and their passengers.

After traveling for two days they arrived at their destination. They could see the house out in the field just across a shallow ditch. They wanted to arrive with no prior announcement, so they decided to try and ford the ditch. It didn't work; the Model T was stuck. Now they had no choice but to expose their surprise and go to the house for help to get the car dislodged. With the assistance of two fine farm horses the little car was quickly extracted from the mud. A happy reunion followed.

Eventually Opal and her new husband, Ted, settled in Las Vegas, Nevada, when the city was just beginning to gain recognition as a resort center. They worked in the gaming rooms and earned $12 daily paid in silver dollars. That kind of income was unheard of in Adair County, Missouri. They were rich! We were often benefactors of their good fortune.

Every Christmas Opal sent the most exciting box of goodies one could imagine. The gift box contained a special item for each person and in addition, candy, cookies and fruit. One unforgettable treat came in the form of animal-shaped cookies dipped in chocolate then decorated with brightly colored candy sprinkles.

Intermittently throughout the year, she sent boxes of lovely slightly used clothing. Ma made over the things that didn't fit and sometimes we sold or traded items we knew would fit someone else in the community.

Actually, Opal's life had not always been so blissful. She had married an older, previously married man when she was only 16 and had lived a hard life as a farm wife and mother on the South Dakota plains. She had made a tough decision to leave her deteriorating marriage and her two young sons behind. She met Ted when she was trying to find meaning for her life and also was able to regain the respect of her sons.

Some of our most dearly loved friends were not related, but good neighbors. Pet and Grant were a prosperous middle-aged farm couple who had known Ma since she was a young girl. They were some-times critical of our behavior but always kind and thoughtful. Pet made dresses and underslips for me and shirts for the boys. She often came with a birthday cake to celebrate our birthdays. Because she taught my Sunday School class it was not unusual for her to take me along to meetings away from our home church. Once she made me a beautiful white cotton dress with a flowing sash and took me with them to the Association all-day meeting.

Pet was a large woman, jolly, yet a hard worker. She wore striped

*Opal and Ted, our 'rich' Las Vegas
relatives with Marine son, Elmer.*

Uncle Forest has a good job, too

denim coveralls and accompanied her husband in all the farm
chores—haying, wood-cutting, and caring for the livestock.

Grant did errands for us in town. Sometimes he took the boys with
him on his weekly trading trips.

Their grown-up daughter had left behind an attic full of toys. When we went over to visit Pet and Grant we anticipated an invitation to go upstairs and play with the vast array of great playthings.

Rosie Yadon was really Ma's closest friend. She possessed a subtle sense of humor, too. Once when she came to clean house when Ma was ill, she found an assortment of old shoes under the bed. With nary a flicker of an eyebrow, she declared, "I cook beans with old shoes, don't you?"

We snickered and whispered, "The beans must taste horrible. I hope she doesn't try cooking any for us." It wasn't until after she left that Ma explained, "Rosie burns the old shoes in the cookstove. She doesn't add them to the beans."

When we lived at the Sullivan place our next door neighbors were the Byrds. The household was comprised of three generations: Sally, her two sons Willard and John, and John's son, Roy. Strange that we called them all by their first names, but that is the way it was then. Sally was the most delightful soul I've ever known. Her hair was shining silver with highlights of gold, and her face seemed always to be pleasant and smiling. She kept their four-room house neat and clean for her sons and grandson. John's wife had died when Roy was a child and Willard was not yet married.

Roy, who was probably in his 20s owned a fine new Willys Knight sport coupe. He often loaded all of us up into his little car and took us to Greentop to the outdoor movies. What a treat! We didn't need any money because the movies were provided free of charge by the local merchants. I can still remember the thrill of topping the little hills on the smooth dirt road on our way to the highway.

On my ninth birthday Velma Houston provided an unforgettable experience. She had sent my name in to a radio show to have the star of the show sing a song especially dedicated to me for my birthday. To make sure I would get to hear it, she invited me over to stay all night and made a special birthday cake for me.

You might suppose Velma was a friend my own age. Not at all. She was older than my mother. But her only son was grown up and gone from home. We shared a great friendship. As I recall, friendship knew no age barriers. We had schoolmates, playmates and acquaintances our own age, but they were not necessarily our closest friends. Our best remembered friends were often older people.

Chapter Ten

Eight to Grow On

Because the farm year ran from March to March and the school year began in late August and ran until mid-April, my brothers, sister and I went to a different school each year and even attended two schools in some years. As a result, even though we were educated in one-room, eight-grade country schools, we had a variety of teachers and got to know a greater number of classmates than if we had remained in one school the entire eight years. With dedicated teachers these humble schools provided a window to the world, however limited the view may have been. My most memorable experiences came from the days spent in the rural Adair County, Missouri schools.

I started school in the fall of 1934 when I was five years old. My first grade teacher, Roy Long, a young man whom I truly admired, instilled in me a great curiosity for learning and a deep respect for those who teach.

In the six years it took me to progress through seven grades, I attended four schools. I began first grade in Bald Knob, moved to the Albert Sullivan place to attend Hungry Hollow in second grade, started third grade at Hazel Creek walking the extra two miles from the Albert Sullivan place for about six weeks until we actually moved into that district. We moved again in my fourth grade to a remote corner of Hungry Hollow District where we lived at the old coal mine house near the highway and the Wabash Railroad. Our next move took us to Sublette in the Gates District where I took sixth and seventh grades. Because these small schools had developed a system of teaching odd-numbered grades five and seven one year and even-numbered grades six and eight the next, I went from fourth to sixth and was never required to take the fifth grade.

A typical rural Adair County School served eight grades with an average enrollment of about twenty students. The teacher, remarkably, kept all students busy most of the time. While the teacher conducted one class, another group prepared for its turn. Older students read stories to younger ones or tutored them with arithmetic, reading or spelling. Art and music involved the whole group.

Most of the schools owned a hand-cranked phonograph and a selection of recordings of marches and classics. One of the upper grade students operated the phonograph, playing "Stars and Stripes Forever," by John Phillip Sousa while all the other students participated in the rhythm band. The rhythm band instruments ran the gamut from sticks to blocks, from triangle to tambourine, all designed to give students a feeling of participation in the great music of Sousa and others. It was a special honor to be chosen as leader or to play the tambourine.

Most of the teachers played the piano and conducted group singing every day. In addition, a traveling music teacher came once a week to teach the "do, re, mi's."

Mrs. Reeves, one of our visiting music teachers, used an ingenious method of helping students express the full range of the scale. One day we practiced with "Here, piggy, piggy, piggy," and on another day it could be "Come chickie, chickie." We learned new songs and sang old favorites. We rehearsed special songs for special occasions. And what's more, we thoroughly enjoyed it. We delighted in performing for our parents and the community.

In 1939 when we attended Gates School we traveled by bus to Kirksville to compete in a music contest with all the other rural schools in Adair County. The first bus trip for most of us, the day-long excursion afforded our first glimpse of the city. Our thoughtful teacher made provisions for a picnic lunch with fresh fruit and cheese as special delights.

Although the variety of media for the expression of art was somewhat limited, we gained an appreciation for art in spite of the limitations. The teacher displayed large full color prints of the classic works, such as "Blue Boy," "Whistler's Mother," and "The Gleaners" before the entire school room. She gave the details of the history of both the artist and the work. She asked questions and invited questions and comments. After a thorough discussion of the art work of the day, the students were invited to draw a facsimile of a model drawing placed at the front of the room by the teacher.

We knew then that my younger brother Robert would some day be an artist. His drawings excelled even the upper level students. Teachers took special delight in his gifted ability. Teachers and students alike were amazed with his perception and creativity.

But the most enjoyable art project that I can remember was not part of our art instruction. On every major holiday we always decorated the blackboard with huge colored chalk murals during lunch hour and recess. After selecting the proper motif for the particular holiday, such as a turkey and pilgrims for Thanksgiving, ghosts and pumpkins for Halloween, or a jolly Santa for Christmas, the teacher chose two of the taller students in school to hold the perforated pattern as close to the top of the blackboard as possible. Several students equipped with dusty chalk erasers then gently patted them over the pattern, careful to cover all the perforations. When the two who had been holding it up removed the pattern, tiny white dots outlined the detail in the turkey or Santa Claus.

As soon as the teacher approved the completion of the pattern application, she assigned two or three boys and girls with artistic ability to fill in the outlines with vibrant color. With the holiday over, we were always a little sad to wash the beautiful designs from the blackboard.

Teachers often fulfilled our creative urges by encouraging us to make craft items as gifts or for our own use. When we attended Hazel Creek, Miss Mildred demonstrated how to make a hot-dish mat on a string loom. I wanted desperately to make one for Ma but I couldn't think of a way to earn the dime needed to pay for materials. Finally, I told Grandma Sevits of my dilemma. She gave me the dime. When I brought the finished product home and proudly presented it to Ma, I was disappointed with her reluctance to accept it. Ma felt I should give it to Grandma when she discovered Grandma had paid for the materials. I understood. Pleased by our thoughtfulness, Grandma placed the snow-white woven-string mat under a beautiful cut glass serving dish and displayed it in a prominent place in her glass-doored china safe.

When we attended Gates School, Milton, Jimmy and I presented an unusual if not unique situation. I had started school a year early and had skipped a grade, making me two years ahead of my con-temporaries. Milton had been ill the year he normally would have started and was held back an additional year, setting him behind two years. Ma had purposely kept Jimmy at home one year to compen-sate for the large difference which would have existed between the two. So, there we were, all three in the same grade sharing the same seat and the same set of books. The problems created by this

SCHOOL DAYS

Milton

James

Roena

Robert

Shirley

Teddy

arrangement soon became obvious. Not the least came from the fact that we could not complete assignments at school and consequently were forced to do most of our school work at home in the evening by lamplight. The fights that ensued over whose turn it was to use which book caused Ma to register a complaint with the teacher.

Mrs. Mildred (she had married since she taught at Hazel Creek) confessed that she had not anticipated the inconvenience that the book sharing would cause at home. After all, she told Ma, there were no problems at school. She explained further that she was simply trying to save money for the already depressed school district. But she did agree to order two more sets of books and to give us separate seats at school.

In that same year we were forced to miss 17 days due to scarlet fever in our family. We were fortunate that Ma got us separate books so we could independently catch up on the studies we missed. Of course, we were not allowed to have our books at home during the quarantine.

It was at Gates School that we began our own hot lunch program. In the colder months when the big coal-burning heater was fired up, we brought ingredients from home for hot soup. The older students took turns peeling potatoes, carrots and onions or sorting and washing dry beans. Each family brought vegetables, a meat bone or milk and butter for the soup of the day. Each student was responsible for keeping his own bowl and spoon clean.

On special occasions such as Christmas or Valentine's Day, we'd chip in a penny or two from each family and buy Jello and bananas for a lovely dessert. I can just see that big blue porcelain mixing bowl filled to the brim with shimmering red gelatin dotted with banana slices. The teachers brought treats for birthdays. We particularly enjoyed the gaily decorated cup cakes in little fluted paper baking cups. We had always called these delightful treats "Jim" cakes. Somehow, quite by accident, we discovered that they were correctly called "gem" cakes, the name being associated with the idea that the little cakes were like rare gems.

Teachers who had taught members of our family agreed that we were among the most eager learners they had taught. We couldn't get our fill of reading. It was one of my most satisfying experiences to be allowed to read stories aloud to the younger students. Somehow *Black Beauty* and *Alice in Wonderland* took on another dimension when the words were audible.

I developed a great love for limericks in the country schools. One set of reference books had a section in each volume that featured nonsense. I can still remember the "old man from Nantucket who kicked the bucket," and the duchess "whose rumblings abdominal were simply abominable." And there were many I have long since forgotten.

Perhaps the best times were associated with extra-curricular activites. We were so poor that Santa Claus never came to our house. But we *knew* he would come to school. Usually a relative or friend of the teacher donned a red suit and white beard and regaled us with gifts and a bag of candy and fruit. We knew the teacher had generously sacrificed to provide this holiday joy, but we felt the spirit of love touching us through the jolly, fat-bellied, red-suited Santa. Because the distribution of gifts and treats usually occurred following the Christmas program, the generosity was not limited to students. Preschool children grew wide eyed as Santa came to each one with his bag of goodies. Parents silently blessed the kindly teacher whose treat filled the void they knew they could not.

The masquerade party at Halloween provided another occasion designed to involve the whole community. One year Ma bought an "Indian maiden" mask for me and a "witch" mask for my little sister, Shirley. I asserted my elder sister rights to force a trade of the masks. I knew I could concoct a witch costume to win a prize. I wasn't too sure about an Indian maiden. I worked hard to make my black costume look authentic. I constructed it from an old black dress someone had given us. I didn't spend as much effort with Shirley's costume, however. But her dark hair and equally dark eyes made her a natural for the Indian maid role. With no effort at all, she won first prize. I sulked a little, but only briefly, because a member of *our* family had won. Ma had been aware of the whole scenario and had said nothing. I think she knew I got the message.

Recess and lunchtime gave us opportunity for participation in group activities. When we played baseball everyone got to bat. Winning or losing somehow didn't seem to matter much. We played for fun and exercise.

The school day began with a flag-raising ceremony followed by calisthenics. The teacher stood at the front of the class and called out, "one, two, three, four," as we jumped, stretched and bent.

In the normal two-mile walk to and from school we developed relationships and shared secrets with school mates that lasted at least until the next school year when we met and made new friends. Somehow no food ever tasted quite as good as lunch pail leftovers shared with school mates on the homeward trek. We were always glad to trade homemade pumpkin pie for peanut butter and crackers or a part of a sandwich made with "baker's bread."

Occasionally we got ourselves into trouble on our walk to and from school. One early spring when the ice had just begun to thaw, we cut across the pond in the same pasture we had all winter. But this time as we reached the middle of the pond, the ice began to heave and sigh giving a rubbery walking surface. A few of us had made it across easily. But we weren't too surprised when the bigger boys, stationed several feet apart jumping up and down in rhythm making the surface spring up and down, caused a huge crack to develop. It sounded like a giant watermelon bursting. Just about that time the cracking sound was accompanied by a resounding, "Kersplash!" Jimmy had fallen in. By the time we fished him out and wrapped him in some of our coats and sweaters, his teeth were chattering. When we got home we got a strong lecture from both Ma and Dad on the hazards of walking on thin ice.

We learned our basic skills—reading, writing and arithmetic—in the country schools. But these schools provided more than just a place for learning. They gave us an appetite for life, an appreciation for the world around us and a glimpse into the universe beyond.

Chapter Eleven

So Dear to My Childhood

William S. Pitts, Iowa hymn writer, shared the feelings of all who grew up in a rural church with these words, "No spot is so dear to my childhood as the little brown church in the vale." These days were dear because events that occurred in these humble places touched lives in ways they would never be affected again.

As I recall the little churches of my childhood, I am somehow filled with a warm glow at the recollection. Hazel Creek Union Church, the church of Grandpa and Grandma Sevits and her father before her who had actually sawed the boards and driven the nails, was the one we always returned to even when it meant walking through mud or snow up to four miles. When we lived too great a distance to walk there, we attended churches at Bald Knob, Low Ground, Green Grove and Sublette.

Generally the physical arrangement was the same. The building itself, always in need of paint, stood close to the road with the cemetery to the side or back. With a high-pitched roof that sheltered one large meeting room heated by a giant coal- and wood-burning heating stove, strategically located in the center, the church provided a refuge for peace-seeking souls.

Though simply appointed with pews hand hewn by my own Great-Grandpa Felker, arranged for optimum utility not only for congregate meetings, but for breaking up into groups for Bible study during Sunday School, the main room served the congregation well. At the front the pastor stood on an elevated platform with a lectern for his Bible and hymn book. To one side stood the piano and on the other, the choir pews. An altar rail extended across the front of the stage with the communion table centered at the front.

For a long time Hazel Creek Church was equipped with two separate doors on the side that faced the road, one for entry and the other for exit. These were later centered in a double door and protected from the weather by an entry hall and coat closet.

Hickory brush clustered around the outdoor toilets to guarantee the privacy of the most modest men and women. Children, bored with lengthy sermons, giggled on their frequent trips to and from the mail-order-catalog-equipped relief stations.

Sunday morning—rain or shine, sleet, hail or snow—brought worshipers from all around the community surrounding the church, to hear a fire and brimstone sermon and to participate in Bible study. The Sunday School superintendent opened the Bible study session with reports of last Sunday's attendance and offering. He invited persons with birthdays to come before the group for recognition. He made pertinent announcements, led in a hymn and then asked someone to pray. Following the opening exercise the congregation broke into smaller groups of men, women and children segregated mostly by age.

We rallied at Jesus' renunciation of the Pharisees' pomposity. We reveled in the triumphs of David, Sampson, Isaiah and Moses. We took great comfort in the fact that we were truly children of God.

Teachers with informal titles—"Delmie" and "Aunt Sylvie"— instilled these immortal messages into us through their teaching as well as their actions. "Delmie" brought lots of cookies. "Aunt Sylvie" gave us little Bibles and carnations on Mother's Day. To make certain the lesson of the day would not be quickly forgotten, each student received a picture card depicting a memorable scene, with a condensed version of the lesson on the reverse side.

For special occasions such as Christmas and Children's Day we rehearsed our programs on weekdays for presentation to the whole congregation. We wore crepe paper costumes and committed our lines to memory. Somehow the role of the dandelion or the sparrow was assigned to me. I really envied the boy or girl who had bright red or yellow costumes for cardinals or roses, while I was stuck with drab brown for a sparrow. But the message made up for the lack of color. After all, beauty soon fades away and further, if God is concerned with the sparrow, is He not even more concerned with the well-being of His children?

In addition to the regular Sunday morning church school and preaching service, every fifth Sunday of any given month gave cause for celebration. The churches of the denomination in a particular district all came together in one church for an all-day meeting with dinner on the grounds, weather permitting. Church women perfected their best recipes to be tasted and praised by all. The men built temporary tables by simply attaching heavy boards from one tree to the next. They built a fire to heat water for coffee or to roast wieners and marshmallows. The basket of every family held such good things as fried chicken, potato salad, baked beans, pickled beets, deviled eggs, fruit salad, hickory nut cake or apple pie. In our wildest dreams we could not imagine more delightful fare. No one missed the fifth Sunday meetings unless he was ill or otherwise incapacitated.

The Easter Sunday Egg Roast provided an occasion for another such food festival. Traditionally, at Hazel Creek Church, following Easter Sunday preaching, everyone gathered in Jim Newcomer's hollow for a pot luck dinner and egg roast. When Easter came early, the big bonfire radiated warmth to sooth chilled bones as well as a place to boil eggs and toast marshmallows.

In 1937 Easter fell on March 28, about the earliest date it can occur. The winter had been a long hard one. Ma had lost her new baby boy and she wasn't feeling very well besides. In spite of her feelings she decided to go to Easter church service and the egg roast to follow. We were glad Ma planned to go. Dad seldom went to church, so Ma knew he wouldn't be going, but he agreed that she needed to get out of the house. She got busy remodeling a dress that her sister Opal had given her and also made certain all the buttons were firmly re-sewn on her coat. There remained but one problem: She had nothing but the shabbiest pair of shoes. Cliff offered the solution to this dilemma. He had just bought himself a pair of canvas shoes out of the mail-order catalog. He hadn't even worn them yet.

"Here, Ma," he said. "Just try them on."

Accepting his offer, Ma tried on the left one, and sure enough, it fit to a T.

"But, Cliff," she protested. "What will you wear?"

"That's simple, Ma. I'm not going."

"All right, son. I'll wear them. You know it is muddy and they are sure to get messed up, don't you?" Ma added.

"Sure, Ma, I know that. But they are canvas and the mud will wash right out," reassured Cliff.

As Easter drew nearer Ma was feeling much worse and besides she thought it more important for 14-year-old Cliff to be with his friends at the Easter egg roast. She had to go into the hospital on March 16. So Cliff tiptoed through the mud with his new canvas shoes. He didn't stay for the ball game after dinner because he promised Dad he would come right home to take care of things while Dad went to the hospital.

On a midsummer evening sandwiched in some time between haying and harvest, the Ladies Home Mission Society sponsored an ice cream social. The men hand turned cranks on the wood-staved freezer pails, while children waited anxiously for a clue as to when the ice cream would be ready. The ladies busied themselves laying out cakes made from their favorite recipes. Because this was their only money making project, the ladies took a free will offering. The offering, of course, was meant to underwrite the expenses of missionaries in the field.

One such missionary was Reverend T. H. Willy. When Brother Willy brought his movies from remote mission outposts in Colombia and Panama, the church was filled to capacity. As he cranked the battery-lighted projector we watched wide-eyed while the parade of South American Indians passed before us. What a sight to behold! What a benevolent service to work among the primitive people in South America! No amount of preaching by itinerant evangelists could equal the example of Brother Willy's love in action.

But the evangelists were also an integral part of the rural church life. They came regularly and held revival meetings. Grown men, coarse looking from hard work, fell to their knees in tears and repented of their sins. Children, somewhat terrified by the prospect of eternal hell fire, came forward and professed their faith.

A unique spin-off of the evangelistic meetings—held outdoors in a clearing in the woods—was the brush arbor meeting. Independent evangelists trying to reap a few souls and a little cash, with the help of some of the men in the community, cleared the brush, built some crude benches and set up an altar. People came from far and near to hear the pickin' and singin' and a call to repentance.

Baptism followed the evangelistic services when souls had been won to the Lord. In the icy waters of the Chariton River, Brother Jim Miller baptized Ma on February 8, 1922.

The cemetery, situated on the gentle slopes behind the church, provided a resting place for members and nonmembers alike. The men of the community dug the graves and kept the grass cut. On every Decoration Day Grandpa Sevits distributed American flags to the graves of military veterans. The flags took on a rather grand flair fluttering among the brightly blooming peonies and wild daisies.

Brother Jim Miller, hip deep in the icy waters of the Chariton River, baptizing the converts, February 8, 1922

As long as I live I shall cherish the memories of the church of my childhood.

Chapter Twelve

We Build the Men to Fit the Clothes

Sixteen-year-old Cleo learned about the CCC Camp program
from another boy in the community who had already joined.
Excited, he begged permission from Ma and Dad to sign up. He
could earn $25 per month for the family and $5 for himself. He had
heard that one might be sent to California to fight forest fires and
floods. Reluctantly, Ma and Dad agreed to let him sign up for a
six-month hitch.

He worked in gravel pits and on building projects. He lived a
regimented life and wore old World War I uniforms. For Cleo and
most of the boys participating in the CCC Camp program, this
experience provided their first long-term away-from-home slice of
life. But they were well fed and they learned new skills.

Most of the boys had no more than eighth grade education, so any
skills they learned in camp would be useful when they got out. Many
failed to complete the six months and were given dishonorable
discharges. Cleo stayed two hitches. He wanted to sign up for a third
hitch, but Ma objected fervently. It was Dad who persuaded him,
though, with the argument that unless he returned home Dad would
not be permitted to work on WPA.

Rather than try to tell about the CCC Camp from my own
recollections, I will let Cleo's letters home and the letters from our
family speak for themselves. The exchange begins with a post card,
our first word from Cleo from the camp at Canton, Missouri.

Note: Letters are set exactly as originally written.

Wed., March 31, 1937
Dear Folks: I will drop you a line or so. You don't need to be worried about me as I am making it all right. You don't write to me
till I write again as they aim to take me to Fort Ellevensworth

(Leavenworth), Kans. and from there to Oregon, Calif. or Wash. I don't know which. I like it fine here. All the officers are nice guys. My left arm sure is sore. I took a shot in it the day I came. We are one mile west of Canton. I can see the Mississippi from here. I may not write for a week.

Goodbye,
Cleo May

Sat. 10, 1937 April
Folks

I guess I won't get to go to Cal. Capt. got a telegram saying not to send us until he got other orders. I sure hate it because we didn't get to go. Has Ma come home or not! How is she anyway? I got a new pair of shoes, underwear, shirt and O.D. pants. You fellows can write but don't send anything til I find out if I am going to stay.

I like it all right around here. We had a big dance here last night. I have got to get me a locker. They cost $3.25. Has Gene and Beulah gone back or not. Well, I guess that is about all.

Cleo Thomas May

Monday, April 12
Dear Folks:

I want you to take that yellow box I have in my tool box and put everything in it in something else. Send me the box with some soap, a towel, my toothbrush, and tooth powder, and if you can think of something else like that I might need. Well, I am making it all right. Two boys went over the hill this morning. Has Ma got out of the hospital or not? I guess I will stay here. This evening will be the first time we will go to the field. When you write, send some paper and a stamped envelope.

Cleo T. May

The next envelope contains two letters to Cleo, one from Ma and one from Dad.

Greentop, Mo., April 16, 1937
My Dear Noble Son:

Well, I finally got released from the hospital after being there 24 days and then they sent me to Sherman's from Sat. till Thursday and then the 15th they let me come home. I sure was glad to get home and the kids were glad to see me, but I am getting along so slow but I ought to be thankful I am alive for the doctor told me lots of times that he didn't think I would live. And let me tell you who is in the hospital now. Can you guess? It's Wendell. He was operated on last Monday and getting along fine. He had appendicitis and his appendix wasn't ruptured but it would have been if they hadn't got him there when they did. I want you to be a good boy and if you get sick you must tell them you are sick so they will take care of you. If you stay there, your Dad and I will come over and see you when we get some money.

I am sending you a stamp so you can write and just as soon as I get some money I will send you some. I am so tired I must quit. Be sure and tell me if you get your box. So goodbye and good luck and write me a letter and tell me all about the camp.

> Your mother,
> With lots of love.

Greentop, Mo., April 17, 1937
Mr. Cleo May, Canton, Mo.
Dear Son:

I will try and write you a few lines to let you know we are all very well. I have planted most of my early garden. I have been so busy. I should have wrote you sooner but I had Beulah write you. We sent your things you wanted yesterday. Your Mother is home but getting along slow.

I hope you are contented there in camp. They probably will send you somewhere else before long. I will send you some money as soon as I can.

We are supposed to get another grant about May 1st. I saw Sol May, my brother and he said for you to write to him: 519 West Wellington St., Waterloo, Iowa. So don't forget it. Well, Cleo, be a good boy and remember I am proud of you. Make up your mind to stay, though it may get a little lonesome for you time goes by pretty fast and it will be a great education and make a man of you.

I will close for this time as your Mother is going to write, too.
Goodbye and good luck,
Your father, Thomas May

Sunday 18, 1936(7)
C.C.C. Camp
Dear Folks:

I got the soap, towel and things all right. I sure was glad to get them. They will give us things like that as soon as they can get them. We have went over across the river to work two times now. We ride the ferry in the morning, but it is too windy to come back across at evening so we go to Quincy to cross. Sure is some ride. I like it alright here but when you go to work you have to keep right on moving till it is time to quit. You can't rest on the job. We work six hours a day. We don't have to work on Sat. unless it rains some day in the week. It rained here Monday so we had to work Sat.

They aim to take 18 boys to Troy, Missouri Monday. I may be in that bunch. Do NOT mistreat Tony (his dog); and don't let anyone fool with my rifle or Bike. I sure wish I had my bike here. We have to dress in army clothes for supper every night. We haven't got our oversea caps but soon will. Some of us boys went down to the dam last Sunday. Has Ma come home? Are you guys making garden? There is some of the finest rye and wheat over in Illinois you ever saw.

We have to take a mess kit with us to the field every day we work. A truck brings some grub from camp about noon. We start to work at 8:00 and quit at 2:30. We are clearing levees. They asked me if I could cut hair and I cut a guy's hair to show them and they said they would set up a barber shop and give me and another guy the job. We will charge 20¢ and give 5¢ to the camp. One guy in here had hair growing down the back of his shirt collar. Now that is the truth. So the Captain said it would be all right to cut his hair if we do a good job. So some of the boys held him and I cut his hair. He sure did have a cat fit. His last name is St. Clair, but everyone calls him "Whiskers." He sure is some guy.

Well, I guess that is about all I can think of right now. Take this
letter to Grandma's and let her read it and if Ma hasn't come
home, take it to her. Well, that is all.

>   Cleo May
>   C.C.C. Co. 3736
>   Canton, Mo. D-I-M

Tell everybody to write.

Greentop, Mo., April 21, 1937
My Dear Son—

We got your letter yesterday and was glad as usual to hear from
you. Hope you are O.K. I don't feel a bit good. My back hurts all
the time but maby I will soon get to feeling better. Tom had lots
of the garden made when I came home and it's all coming up
now. We had a fine rain yesterday and the grass and everything is
sure growing. Clifford is going to wash today. Your suit is up to
Grandma's and I'm going to have Clifford to take your bicycle up
there soon as the roads dry up and lock it up. Have you seen
Nathan yet? He left Kirksville Monday for camp. I don't believe
he will stay long.

Say, Cleo, how would it suit you to let Ted have that gun back
and then you can buy you a good gun when you come home. If
you want to do that you tell me when you write and I'll do as you
say about it. I am glad you got you a barbering job. You can make
some money.

I am sending you some stamps and you can write any time.
There isn't any news to tell you so you write me a big letter and
tell me all the news. You tell me about the gun and I'll do what
you say. Hope you get along with the boys and officers and especially Whiskers. Please don't get into the habit of smoking for your
Dad worries me to death with his old pipe. My back hurts so I
will have to quit.

>   From your Mother

P.S. When you write tell me what kind of grub you have to eat.
Write soon. Don't worry about Tony for he is fatter than I am. He
sure is getting all he wants to eat, but he misses you.

*Cleo the rookie
in a fine World
War I uniform*

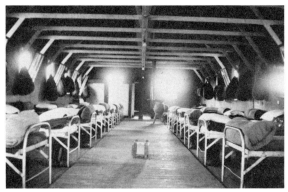

Barracks #2, Camp Company 3771, Troy, Missouri

Troy, Missouri, April 20, 1937
Dear Mother and Family:
I was sent to Troy, Mo., last night. 17 other guys came with me.
I am in barracks No. 2, Camp Co. No. 3771. I was issued a complete outfit of clothes and a C.C.C. issue kit. I am about 60 miles
from St. Louis. If I knowed where Sylvia lived I would go over
there some weekend. How are all of you folks? I am feeling O.K.
How are you, Mother? The hills are all green with grass down
here. This is a lot better camp than the one at Canton but they are
strict as the devil. I think I can make it all right here for six
months. You folks don't need to worry about me for I am not
going to get into any trouble as long as I am in this camp.

The camp is a way back in the woods. It is about five miles north of Troy.

I may get sent from here before long as this is more or less a breaking in camp to get boys ready for the west coast and Arkansas. Although there are a lot of men who have been here a long time and expect to stay their time out.

Thanks a lot for the stamps. Tell Clifford I was glad to get his letter.

This sure is a big camp. Fixed up nice and all that. There is woods all around this camp. I don't know how hard the work is as I haven't worked in this camp. One thing I am glad of that is we don't have to use a mess kit. We will be close to camp and can come to the mess hall to eat. They carry out the army rules more here than they did up to Canton.

Well, I can't think of any more to write, so will stop.

                                        Cleo T. May

Use address on letter.

C.C.C. Co. 3771
Troy, Missouri
April 27, 1937
Dear Mother and Family:

I haven't received an answer to my last letter but I suppose it hasn't had time to get there yet. As I said before I have been sent to Troy. I am sorry I didn't get to see Nathan.

I have worked in a gravel pit for the last three work days and I may work there all summer. It isn't easy either.

You asked me in the letter you wrote to Canton what I had to eat there but I will tell you what we have to eat here. I can't tell everything because we have almost everything you might think of. One morning we had honey and pancakes. We have potatoes every day. Well, I can't tell you everything but I sure have all I want to eat.

You asked me about that gun. Sure I want you to take that gun back. I gave Ted 3 days work for the gun and I owe him $1.30. He ought to be glad to take the gun back for I had it fixed better than it was. By the way, the first check will only be $20.00 as I will be 6 days short of a month. One dollar will be taken out of my

$5.00 and I drawed a $1.00 canteen book. And that will leave me
only $3.00 pay day. A canteen book is worth a dollar in trade at
the canteen.

I wish you would try to sell my bike for $4.50 as I will have to
buy a locker and it will cost $4.50. If anybody says they will buy
it, don't let them ride the wheels off from it trying it out.

Dad said to write Sol, so I did. How is Grandma and Grandpa
feeling? I have begun to like it here by now. I have got a complete outfit of clothes now. This camp is in a park of 5600 acres.

Are you feeling better Ma? Let Grandma and Grandpa read this
letter, too. Tell Grandma that I was glad to get her letter. Well, I
guess that is all. Good bye.

Cleo T. May

P.S. I am about 150 miles from Kirksville.

Sun. evening

Dear Mother and Family:

How are all of you making it? I am feeling O.K. I done a washing today. It has been rainy all day. We got rained out two days
last week but didn't have to make it up on Sat. for it was in
another month. Every month has to take care of itself, so we
didn't have to work Sat.

We had ice cream for dinner today. We will get payed Monday.
I got a card from Ted and Lola.

The C.C.C. boys has to build a road this summer in the Park. I
suppose I will get to shovel my share of gravel. The Camp has
several dump trucks to move dirt with on the road work.

Of all things you should have been here when we had a fire
drill. Some of the officers told a guy to give out a fire alarm with
the fire dong. We didn't know but what it really was a fire and
every man in the camp went to his barracks and got fire buckets
and sand buckets and rushed to the place they said the fire was at.
When we got there they had a little fire built on the ground.

They claim the Ozarks are rocky but you don't have to go that
far, for there are more rocks here than I ever saw before.

We have longer hours here than we had up to Canton. We
worked six hours at Canton and seven here. One thing about these
camps you have all you can eat. The supply sergeant burnt up

some of the best wool jackets you nearly ever saw. The reason
they wouldn't give them to the boys was the boys would take
them and trade them in for new ones.

How is Grandma and Grandpa feeling? Well, goodbye.

> Cleo T. May
> C.C.C. Co. 3771
> Troy, Missouri

P.S. Yes, both of the Williams boys is at camp. Arthur is here and
the other one is Canton. Leland Billington is here—I know him.
He is Harlen Lay's wife's brother. Yes, I got the letter and stamps.

Greentop, Mo.
May 13 - 37
Mr. Cleo May, Troy, Mo.
Dear Son,

Will write you a few lines to let you know we are all well
except your Mother. I took her back to the Hospital today for a
few days so they could look her over. She is not getting along very
well.

We got your first check the 11th and it was for $21.00. How do
you like it down there? You will have to take care of yourself and
don't work too hard especially when it gets hot weather. They
don't expect you to kill yourself and the work you are doing is real
hard work.

Why didn't you answer my letter I wrote you? You never
mention my name in any of the letters I read.

I worked for Ted Sevits and paid him the $1.30 you owed him.
I took the gun back for I didn't think it was worth 3 days work.
We will try and buy you a Winchester shot gun before you come
home.

My garden looks nice. We have had plenty of rain so far.

Your Uncle Bub May died a few days ago. I will write you
again soon to tell you how your Mother is. You won't need to
write her at the Hospital for she will be home in a few days. Well,
I will close. Write me a long letter and tell all about the camp.

> Your Father
> Thomas May

(Over)
Don't worry any about your Mother. If she gets bad we will send

you the money to come home on. I think she will get along all right. It takes a long time for anyone to feel good again after they have been as sick as she was. I will find out what Sylvia's address is in St. Louis. Maby you can go over and see her.

May, Thurs., 13, 1937
Dear Mother and Family:

Why haven't you folks wrote before now, this will make the 3rd letter I have wrote without getting a letter.

Are any of you folks sick or something?

I worked in the gravel pit today and I am pretty tired right now. All the trees are leafed out now.

Me and some other boys went to the river a swimming Sunday. We went up the river along a bluff and it got so steep we couldn't find a place to take our clothes off. The bluff was pure rocks that was straight up and down. I seen more lizards in them rocks than I ever saw before.

How is you guys' garden coming by now? I suppose you folks are wondering why you never got my check yet but I can explain that. We got red lined or in other words, put off our pay till last Sat. because we came in the middle of the month. We got payed Sat. so the other check is more than likely there at the time I write this letter. It will only be $20.00 this time, but it will be $25.00 after that.

What does Tony do since I am gone? I bet he sure does howl. Ha! Ha! I got a letter from Grandma and Grandpa a while ago and answered it. Couldn't you sell the bike?

I will have to go to class in about a half hour. I am going to ask something of you I don't aim to do but just this one time. I wish you would send me $2.00 as I need it to pay on a locker.

I bought a second hand one and owe two dollars on it and I want to take my check and buy a new one as one won't hold all of my clothes. If I don't get the two dollars the guy I bought it from will take it back. This will be the only time I aim to send after money. But I do wish after this month you would put $10.00 a month in the bank for me for if you knew how hard I work for this money you wouldn't fall back a bit from putting $10.00 a month in the bank. That would be $50.00 when I come home.

Now you know it would be the devil to work six months and not get at least that much. The rest I don't care what you do with it.

Well, I guess I will close for this time and I want you guys to write right away.

>   Goodbye,
>   Cleo T. May

Post card dated May 18, 1937

Dear Dad,

I am sorry I haven't written to you. But I send my letters as much to you as I do to anyone else. I would write a letter but I haven't any stamp nor no money to buy one with. I wrote you a letter a day or so ago before I got your letter. I wish you would be sure and do what I said for you to do in my letter. How is Ma? Is she home yet? Please write soon.

>   Cleo T. May

Wed. 18, 1937
Dear Mother and Family:

I received your card Tue. but I never did get a letter with a dollar in it. I asked the 1st Lt. but he acted like he didn't care much. I wrote home Sat. for $2.00 as I need it to pay for a locker I bought.

I will need my $5.00 to buy a new locker with as one won't hold all of my clothes. I don't aim to make a practice of writing for money but I really need $2.00.

I don't know what could have happened to that letter with the money in it unless the guy that handles the money here lost it.

I am glad you are feeling better now. I wrote a post card last night; you may get it the same day you get this.

Well, there is not much to write about. Everything is the same. I am still working in the gravel pit. I will write Dad a line and close.

>   Goodbye

Dear Dad,

I received your letter and was glad to hear from you. I wrote you a card last night, but I got a card from Ma today saying she sent me a dollar, but I never did get it. So I borrowed a stamp and wrote to you.

I wish you would send me that $2.00 I wrote about if you haven't already sent, as I will need it.

We was working in the gravel pit in the creek today when all of a sudden a gush of water came and the creek raised 2 feet in five minutes and not a cloud in the sky. It sure beats me.

Well, I guess I will close as everything is O.K. with me. I will have to have some stamps if I write any more.

> Goodbye,
> Cleo T. May

Greentop, Mo.
May 22, 1937
My Dear Son—

Tom just now came in and brought me your letter and card and I am so mad I don't know what to do to think you never got your money. I wanted to make you feel good and now we are both mad. What do you think became of it? When we send you the $2.00 we will send a money order and then if you don't get it maby you can find out who did. I don't know anything to write for I have been here over a week. I am feeling lots better. I want to go home today. I don't know if they will let me out or not but I am sure sick of this place. I hope you are O.K. and I will get you some money as soon as I can. We are in one awful predicament but I suppose we will get used to it.

Jimmie is staying with Beulah as Gene went back to Waterloo and she don't aim to go back. Milton and Roena went up to your Grandma May's but just as soon as I get out of here I am going to bring them home. What is worrying me now is that I will be O.K. when they turn me loose. I sure don't like the idea of giving my checks to the doctor. But if I ever get my health back I won't regret it. I had planned on getting lots of things.

Well, I must close. I am sending you some stamps this time. I hope you get them and please write right back.

Send your letter home for I surely will go home soon. If I don't
get to go today. I am lots better than I was when I came in here. I
was afraid they would have to operate again.

                                    Write Soon
                                    Your Mother

May 26, 1937
C.C.C. Co. 3771, Troy, Mo.
Dear Mother,

I got your letter yesterday and was glad to hear from you. It
sure came a real rain here late yesterday evening. This surely will
be a crop year. I worked on the road today loading trucks.

I am feeling o.k. and I hope you are the same. Have you come
home yet or not? I suppose Dad has a nice garden. How is
Grandpa and Grandma? Are they O.K.? I believe I have changed
my mind about selling my bike. If you have already sent it up to
Grandma's leave it up there till I come home. When you get the
money to spare I want you to send my bathing suit to me. I will
get payed next Monday and the other check will get home about
ten days later. I owe all my money but 40¢ so I won't have much
to spend.

We go to bed about 10:00 and get up at 6:00. We have to make
our bed, sweep out the barracks and clean up for breakfast before
7:00 as we have breakfast at 7:00. We have work call at 8:15.

I wish that from now on you would put $10.00 a month in the
bank so I would have $50.00 when I come home. I asked about it
before, but you never said if you would do it or not. I sure wish
you would try to do that because if I stayed here six months and
came home and didn't have at least that much it sure would be
HELL. That would leave $15.00 a month for you. That is quite a
bit and you could do anything you want with it.

I asked the lieut. about the letter with the money in it but he
said there wasn't anything he could do about it. He said I better
have money registered. We have 1st and 2nd Lieut., Captain and
1st Sergeant for officers. The 1st Lieut. is officer in command.

Well, I guess I will close. Tell Dad and all the kids I said Hello.
                                    Goodbye,
                                    Mr. Cleo T. May

(A post card from Dad dated May 27, 1937)

Dear Cleo:

Will write you a few lines. We brought your Mother home but I
am going to take her back to the Hospital soon as she really needs
to be in the hospital. We hope you are satisfied down there.
Nathan Yadon came back home to stay. It was too tough for him.
Cleo, I hope you wasn't mad at us for not sending you the $2.00 to
finish paying for your locker but we are living awful hard now as
we have to pay the Hospital so much.

But we have a real good garden and it won't be long until we
will have plenty of garden stuff and won't need to buy so much.
Please write as often as you can, especially to your dear Mother.

                              Your Father, Thomas May

P.S. We had a 3 inch rain here yesterday.

May 31, 1937, Monday
Dear Mother,

I will write you a line to let you know I am alright. We got this
Monday off but I had to work K.P. today. K.P. is kitchen police.
Everybody takes their turn on weekends, but during the week
they have regular K.P.

If I can get enuff money I aim to come home the 4th of July. It
is so hot I can't hardly write.

You know those stamps you sent me, well I put them and three
more on envelopes and put them in my locker, but it got so hot
they all stuck together.

We had ice cream for dinner today and yesterday.

This camp's ball team played Eoila Sunday and beat them 6 to
7. It sure was a tight game.

Well, I guess I will have to stop as I can't think of anything to
write. How are you feeling Ma? Have you come home yet? I
hope you are alright. Mother I don't want you to worry about me
as I am alright. Tell Dad and all the kids Hello.

                              Your Son,
                              Cleo T. May

P.S. We will get payed Tuesday.

Sun. evening, Greentop, Mo.
May 30, 1937

My Dear Son—

   I will write you a few lines in answer to your letter we got Sat. I
am over to Cyrus's and I have been for a week. If it hadn't been
for Sylvia taking care of me we would have been paying $3.00 a
day for a Hospital bed. But thank God I got to come out here. I
am getting sick of the hospital. I just now got back from town. I
had to go to see the doctor again today. There was pus around the
kidney and it would have been a dangerous operation. So they
gave me medicine to draw it out and bring it to the surface like a
boil. So sure enough it did and I went and had it lanced and now I
am getting along o.k. I am going to stay here yet this week so I
can get straightened up before I go home. Tom says our garden is
fine. Yes, Cleo we will do what you said about saving you some
money. I never seen the other letter you wrote about it for I was
in the Hospital then. I am so weak I can scarcely walk alone. I
can't tell you the suffering I have gone through with. But I believe
I am going to come out of it now.
   Hope you are fine. Oh say, Nathan left the camp and came
home to stay. I guess he wasn't used to the work. Cleo is it against
the rules to send boys money or not? I don't see how that letter
could have got lost I sent you.
   Wendell is just fine over his operation. He plows and everything. Everything looks fine here but we have been getting a lot of
rain. Beulah is real sick. They sent a telegram for Gene and Forest
brought him home last night and they are getting ready to operate
on her. Daisy and Dewey are living in Farmington, Mo. and
Mother said they were going to move to Illinois today. What did
you ever do with your clothes you wore from home?
   Cleo, honey, I must quit. I am so tired. I'll see that you get your
money. We have an awful Hospital bill before us. So write soon. I
will send you some spending money soon as I get my check. I just
got $21.00 the first time. Sylvia said to tell you Hello. They sure
have been good to me. Write soon.

Mother

P.S. Grandma isn't well. She has Rheumatism.

June 2, 1937
Troy, Mo.
Dear Mother,

I received your letter today so I thought I would ans. it. I wrote you a letter yesterday. I am glad you are out of the hospital.

You asked me if it was against the rules to send money to me. Well, I don't know but there isn't a boy in 3771 who doesn't get from 5 to 25 dollars a month from home. So you can see for yourself. Even the Lieut. said if I had any money sent to me to have it registered and if it is alright with him it ought to be alright with everybody, for he is the commanding officer.

If you want me to come home the 4th you can send a little money and I will take care of it till then. Otherwise you don't have to send it.

Well, I took my last shots last nite. The last ones were for spinal meningitis. I like it alright here and am getting along O.K. I am glad Dad's garden is getting along O.K.

I am getting ready to go to town to the show tonite. I worked loading trucks with dirt today.

What is the matter with Beulah? How are the kids? Has Clifford killed very many squirrels? You don't know what I would give to be home and go squirrel hunting with old Tony. By the way, how is old Tony? I bet he misses me. ha! ha! Well, I miss him as bad.

Well, I guess I will close. Oh, say, you tell Opal if she has any more shirts or anything like that I sure can sell it to the boys as every one of them always wants to buy something like that. Well, I guess I will close. Tell Dad and the kids Hello.

Cleo T. May

P.S. It just got through coming a big rain. Answer soon. It was too bad about Nathan, but I thought it all the time.

Monday morning, Greentop, Mo., June 7, 1937
My Dear Son Cleo—

I am still at Cyrus's and yesterday they took me over to Mother's to spend the day and Tom brought the kids up and we all had a good time but poor little Shirley cried because I didn't go home with her. I am getting lots better now and Wendell says I am getting fat. I sure am poor. You scarcely would know me but if I keep on getting better I'll gain fast when I do start. It's been almost three months since I have been operated on and I have been all this time getting over it. That pus on my kidney almost got me but they are bringing me out of it. I hope you are well and don't never work when you don't feel good or I mean if you feel real sick. Cleo, dear child, you surely know I want you to come home for the 4th and I'll try to send you the money. You know we have had an awful lot of bills pile up on us. Dr. Grim handed me one Sat. for $33.20 and besides I gave him the first check I got.

Wendell told me to tell you he would give you $4.50 for your bicycle and he wants it real bad. Why don't you sell it and I could send you that money. It will be a long time before you would get to ride it. You write right back and tell me if you will sell it and he has the money to buy it with.

The crops here look fine. It rains a little every few days. Everything is sure growing. There is lots of bugs, though. Tom was looking for another grant check but I guess we won't get it. If I can ever get straightened up so your Dad can get away and get work, it won't be so bad.

Beulah was operated on last week. She had an abcess in the rectum. She sure suffers but she will get to leave the Hospital right away. That is if she gets along like she should. Tom is supposed to come over today and help with the alfalfa but he hasn't got here yet.

Well, dear child, I must quit. My back is hurting and I want to write Opal a letter. You be sure and write right back and tell me about the bike for he wants it.

Jake gave Grandpa and Grandma $2.00 each yesterday and told them to buy themselves a new hat. Well I must quit. Write real soon.

Your Mother

June 8, 1937, Troy Mo.
Dear Mother,

I received your letter today and was glad to hear you are as well as you are. I am making it alright, but the weather is pretty warm. I have been working at loading trucks with dirt for the last week.

Yes, it will be alright to sell Wendell the bike. If he buys it, hunt up all bike parts and give them to him.

We have started to have retreat now every Mon., Tue., and Thurs. We have to go up to the flag pole as soon as we hear retreat call and line up double row, to the left of our leader. When the Lieutenant yells attention we all stand straight and look forward. At the command "left dress" we put our left hand on our hip and look towards our barracks leader. Then at the command "left turn" we turn to the left. Then they take the flag down while the officers salute it. Then he says, "March" and we march to the mess hall two abreast. It isn't hard to do after you get on to it. But your teeth has to be clean and your face shaven, socks on, shoes shined, clean clothes and everything.

If Wendell buys the bike send me the money in a registered letter or buy a money order. I will try to come home the 4th if we get Monday off, but if we don't, I don't know whether I could come home and back in a weekend or not.

We have milk two times a day and some kind of cereal every morning. Just to give you an idea of what we have to eat I will name what we had for dinner. Coffee, bread, beans, potatoes, lettuce, sliced tomatoes, spare ribs, butter and coconut pudding. But that was a very light meal to what we generally have.

I mentioned in another letter about you sending me my bathing suit. I wish you would send it as a truck goes to the creek every evening and I haven't anything to wear. Well, I must close.

Your Son,
Cleo T. May

Novinger, Mo., June 10, 1937 (Post card from Aunt Lola)
Dear Cleo—We were so glad to hear from you. Have been so busy or would have ans. sooner. Gardens and fields keep us busy. Ted is plowing corn this morning. Tomorrow he's going to start cutting alfalfa. There are worlds of grasshoppers, most any kind of insect pest one could ask for. I have about 80 baby chicks. They're looking real nice. Gm'a Sevits says you're coming back for the 4th. That'll be nice. Hope we get to see you. How long can you stay? Your Mother is still over to Cyrus's. She's been sick a

long time. Doesn't look very good yet. Do you have to work hard
and do you like the camp as well as you did in the beginning? I'm
hoping so. Guess you knew Nathan came back. Write soon.

                                        Ted and Lola

Greentop, Mo., June 15, 1937
My Dear Son—

I will write you a few lines as I'm sending you $4.50 this morn-
ing and I'm also sending you your bathing suit. Now Cleo answer
right back and tell me if you get it.

Cleo try to get your officers to let you come for a week and if
they won't let you stay a week this time I'd see when they would
and wait till then. Maby if you would tell them how terrible sick I
have been and am yet they would surely let you come. My back is
hurting awful again this morning. I have had 3 months of it now
and I'm sure getting about enough of it.

Beulah and I are both at Mothers. I don't know how long I will
stay but not much longer.

Cleo I am going to ask you a question and please answer it. Do
they allow the boys to gamble in the camp where you are?
Nathan told Tom that they did where he was at Kahoka and sold
beer and I don't know what all. Please tell me when you write. He
got a discharge last week. I suppose it was a dishonorable one.

Well, Cleo honey, I must quit. My back sure is hurting this
morning. I do hope you can come home for the 4th. I know I
would feel better if I could see you. Please answer just as soon as
you get this. Hope you are O.K. Mother and Dad are all right.
Beulah is feeling pretty good.

                                        Your Mother

Friday 1937 (Postmark Troy, Mo., June 26, 1937)
Dear Mother,

I received your letter and money for the stamps and I was glad
to here from you. How are you feeling? Have you come home
yet?

It sure is getting hot down here. I have been loading dump

trucks the last week. If it don't rain next week I am going home
for I don't think I will be on K.P. It is so hot I can't write, so I will
close. Tell Dad and all the kids Hello.

Your Son,
Cleo T. May

The correspondence resumes with a letter from Cleo at Troy
dated July 7, 1937. He did come home for the Fourth of July for a
much too brief visit. The whole family including aunts and uncles,
Grandma and Grandpa, cousins and all of us at our home were so
happy to see him. Oh, he looked grand in his uniform. He was so
sophisticated. We asked a million questions. We were so proud. His
homecoming was a great tonic for Ma.

Dear Mother and Dad,

I got back to camp in time for supper Mon. evening. Dewey
wouldn't take a dime for bringing me down here. All the guys in
my barracks made it back by Tue. morning. It sure is hot down
here.

We had a big feed down here for supper last night in honor of
our 200 accident-free days. We had ice cream, candy, peanuts,
beer or soda pop, whichever you wanted, potatoes, cake, cheese,
salad, peas, young fried chicken, gravy, and cigarettes. They had
the same kind of dinner the 4th. Well, I must close.

Good bye,
(Unsigned)

Greentop, Mo., July 10, 1937
My Dear Son Cleo—

I got your letter yesterday and was glad to hear from you. We
are all O.K. Hope you are the same. It has been threatening rain
all week but we haven't got a rain yet. Did Dewey take you into
Troy or the camp or where did he take you? Did you stay all
night at Sol's or where did you stay? Please tell me when you
write. Grandma wants you to write to her. I saw in the paper yesterday where Vic and Blanch have a boy baby born on the 4th.

Cleo, I'm putting some money in the bank for you today. I looked everywhere for your bank book but I couldn't find it. Tom worked for Harry Filkins last week. I have been feeling pretty good. I do hope I get to feeling my old self again.

Well, I will close. Write me a letter and tell me where you stayed all nite Sun. nite.

Your Mother

July 14, 1937, Troy, Mo.

Dear Mother,

I received your letter the 12th. I was glad to hear that you are O.K. I was mighty glad to hear that you put some money in the bank for me.

Yes, I stayed all nite at Sol's. Sol was there and so was Lissie, Vina and Bill.

Dewey brought me to Troy and I got a ride with the Army truck out to camp.

The bank took over the bank book when I got the money so there's no use to look for it.

We had two small rains here in the last three days and it looks like rain now.

A bunch of new boys are coming in the 15th. Maybe we won't have so much work to do in camp on Sat. then for they'll make the new guys do that.

Well, I guess I will close for it's almost too hot to write. I wrote Grandma a card the same day I wrote your letter.

Goodbye and good luck
Cleo T. May

Greentop, Mo., July 16, 1937

Mr Dear Son Cleo—

Got your letter yesterday and was glad as usual to hear from you. We are all well and hope you are the same. I dreamed last nite you were sick but I hope you are O.K. I have begun to feel real good. I walked up to Velma's the other day.

Well, we really got some rain this week. Everything just looks fine but I'm afraid the grasshoppers are going to ruin our garden. Tom got some of that poison mash and it kills a few. Joe came home from Kirksville with Clifford last Sat. and stayed all nite and James went home with him and stayed 2 nites. The nite he was here someone robbed the store in the north end of town.

Cleo I put $10.00 in the bank for you and the bank book was there in the bank and they used it. I will put more in next month, too. I don't know what on earth we would have done if it hadn't been for you going to camp. We couldn't have paid our bills at all and I'm proud of you too for it. Yadon's couldn't hardly stand it to think that you went back to camp and Nathan wouldn't.

Mother had roasting ears yesterday and will can corn tomorrow. I think we will have corn next week. We are still planting beans and Tom says what vines we already have will make 25 bushels.

Did you sell any of your ties? When you write, tell me. You get in too big a hurry when you write. Your letters aren't long enough.

Well, I better quit. I will look for a letter soon. The mail carrier had left Grandma's card in Cyrus's box. I got your letter the next day after you wrote it. It has been two days before I'd get them. Well, goodbye and good luck. Write soon.

Your Mother

July 20, 1937, Troy, Mo.
Dear Folks,

I received your letter and was glad to hear from you and that you are all well. I am making it O.K. and feeling fine. Yes, I sold the ties for 35¢.

It came a real rain Sunday nite. That made the road too muddy to work on so we went to the gravel pit Monday.

About 20 of the camp's truck drivers went down south to an old transient camp and got 19 trucks last week. A transient camp is where old bums stay. I asked one of the boys what kind of grub they had. They said they walked in the mess hall and an old cook that looked like that old cook in "Out Our Way" in the Kirksville Daily gave them a plate and put some meat and hash on it and then poured some dope over it that looked like buzzard puke. The boys said they just scraped it off in the garbage can and walked out.

Arthur Fay Williams and that Billington kid took a transfer to Montana. I would have went too, but they didn't know where they were going when they left.

Ma, I wish you would put money in the bank along as the checks come in and try to have $50.00 in the bank by the time my six months is up. If you will do that I will stay this winter and help you guys along. You know yourself that a fellow ought to have at least $50.00 out of six months hard work.

There is only seven left in this camp out of the 18 that came from Canton.

We had cornbread and buttermilk for supper Monday nite. One guy fainted at retreat Monday evening. I guess his heart was bad. I got a letter from Grandma and Grandpa the other day. I wrote them a card Sat.

You said to write more, well I can't think of any thing to write about for nothing ever happens here.

James Hall out of my barracks got a long distance telephone call saying his dad was sick, so the Lieutenant gave him a leave to go home. He sure is a nice boy and I hope his dad isn't bad. He sure was worried before he left.

Well, I must close for I have run out of news. I bet your truck patch sure looks nice after the rain.

Goodbye and Good Luck
Cleo T. May

Sun. afternoon, Greentop, Mo., July 25, 1937
My Dear Son Cleo—

I was over to Cassie's when your letter came and I never got to write to you last week. We are all O.K. I am getting better all the time. Hope you are fine. I went up to Cassie's last week and got some sewing done. I sure had a good time. We went over to Rosa Wiles and stayed for dinner one day and she had a fine dinner. The twins are just like they used to be. They and Janet and Pansy all have beaus and Bud has a girl. We had another big rain and everything is fine. Ernest Lawrence had out 8 acres of wheat and threshed 213 bushel of fine wheat.

Yes, Cleo, I am going to save you some money. Tom is going to Iowa with Harve and see about work. He has been working in the hay and that gives me a chance to save you some money.

Cleo, they took Joe and Scott and Jim over to Kirksville and questioned them when that store was robbed in Connelsville. Joe sure is bad. He gets drunk every time he goes to town.

I was over to Mrs. Yadon's a while ago and Fern Bell and Mary Ann and the boys were up in the barn loft. I suppose they were playing cards and didn't want Mrs. Yadon to see them. Jess sold his saw mill. They went to Kirksville yesterday and came here to get lard and sugar for dinner today. Mother and Dad went out to Cleve and Juanita's today.

Well, Cleo, there isn't much to write about. Oh, yes, I got a letter from Beulah and she said that a guy came to Forest's filling station and wanted 3 gallons of gas. He gave Forest a ring and watch and wanted $11.00 from Forest and he gave it to him. Forest took the things to the jeweler and they weren't worth but $1.00. He will have to live and learn.

Well, here it is Monday morning and Grandma is here to help wash, so I will have to quit and go to work. Don't worry about the money for I will save it for you. Write soon and tell me how that boy's father got. Harve said this morning that Winnie Royse fell dead yesterday.

Wishing you good luck and good
health, Your Mother

P.S. Dewey was here yesterday with a new Chevrolet car.

Tue. evening, 1937, Troy, Mo. (Postmark July 28)
Dear Mother,

I received your letter and was glad as usual to hear from you. We worked in the gravel pit all last week. This week we have started to hunt field stone to build rock walls along the road banks.

The dentist came to camp yesterday and examined all our teeth. I had pretty good teeth so he won't work on mine until the last.

It sure is cool down here for this time of the year. Next Sat. is pay day.

I bet you had a good time at Rosie's. I got a card from Grandma Monday. I can't think of a thing to write so will close.

Your Son, Cleo

Dear Dad,

I thought I would drop you a line to let you know how I am making it. I am feeling fine. We're not working so hard right now as we are gathering field stone. I hope you get plenty of work this summer. It isn't very hot down here right now. I will come home again the 4, 5, 6 of Sept. as I get those days off. Well, I must close as I can't think of anything to write.

Your Son, Cleo

(Enclosed in this letter is a hand drawn cartoon where the supply sergeant is saying to the rookie after he has complained about the fit of his clothes, "Quiet, rookie. We build the men to fit the clothes in this Army.")

Dear Clifford,

I received your letter and was glad to hear from you. I sure am glad Dad has got a job down to Motter's. We have been gathering field stone this week.

I hope you do get enough money to buy yourself a rifle and shotgun. I don't know whether I can get my leave during duck season or not. I sure hope I can.

I bet you kids has a lot of hoeing to do. I sure do get hungry for a big mess of squirrels or fish.

How is old Tony making it? Does he miss me or not? Well, I must close.

Cleo

Greentop, Mo., Aug. 2, 1937
My Dear Son Cleo—

I will write you a few lines this morning in answer to your letter I rec'd Sat. Was glad as usual to hear from you. We are all fine and hope you are the same. Clifford isn't here to write to you. He went up to Cassie's last Friday to go to the Worthington picnic and he is coming home this morning. Cleo, is it dry and hot down there? I heard someone say yesterday that things were burning up around St. Louis. Boy, it sure did rain here Sat. nite but at Novger it never rained much and at Kirksville it poured. We sure don't need any rain for a while. When you come home we will have some shells and you can go hunting. Clifford never goes hunting. He is always busy at something. Tom never had any work last week and I don't know if he will have any this week or not. I wish he would go to Iowa. Hershel Hanlin is up there getting $2.50 a day. Het Scott is in the Hospital and I guess she won't get well. She has cancer. Did you find the two stamps I sent you in the other letter? I forgot to tell you I was sending them.

Well, Cleo, I will close. I have to write to Beulah and it's getting late. Forest and Florence was down last week.

Please write soon and we will all be glad to see you when you come home. Write soon.

Your Mother

August 6, 1937, Troy, Mo.
Dear Folks,

I received your letter and was glad to hear from you. It is getting a little hotter down here right now. We don't need rain very much right here in the park but on south of here they do need rain.

I am making it O.K. and feeling fine. How is your garden stuff looking? When is Ted and Opal coming home? When they come tell them to bring you down here.

The trucks are going to St. Louis Sat. to the ball game. I don't know if I will go or not for I won't have the money to get in. I have $2.00 from pay day but I aim to buy off K.P. with that.

I have been working on the road this week. Where is Dad working now? I can't think of anything to write so I must close.

Cleo T. May
Write soon

Greentop, Mo., Aug. 10, 1937
Dear Son Cleo,

   I got your letter yesterday and was real glad to hear from you. I
looked for a letter Sat. and never got it. I was afraid you might be
sick or something. We are all O.K. now. Clifford was awful sick a
couple of days last week, but he is O.K. now. He was working with
Ted hauling baled hay and I think he got too hot. He is over to
Harvey's now helping Velma. Harve took a load of lumber to
Des Moines for Arthur Scott yesterday.

   They are working on the church now getting ready for the
association the first of next month. They are going to have the
homecoming at Greentop this year on the 1, 2, 3, and 4 of Sept.
Clifford went to the Worthington picnic with Ernest and Cassie
and the kids. Silas Yadon had a fight up there and got his nose
broke.

   Tom is hoeing this morning; he hasn't any work now. He
worked with Harve last week 2 or 3 days. They hauled hay from
Worthington to Kirksville. I want to go to Kirksville today if I can
to put your money in the bank. Well, Cleo, I must close. I want to
string some beans and dry them today. Our beans are fine. The
grasshoppers are awful.

   Cleo, Dewey comes home every 2 wks. and maybe he can
come by and bring you up or take you back, one. I'll send his
address and maby you can write to him and find out. He was
going to bring peaches this weekend but I don't think he came.

   Mother and Dad are O.K.—working every day. Write soon. Just
get you some cards and it will be cheaper for you. I just want to
hear from you and know how you are. I don't care how much you
write. Here is Dewey's address: Mr. Dewey Sevits, Farmington,
Mo. Box 242.

                         Love and Best wishes
                         Your Mother

Friday night 13, 1937, C.C.C. 3771, Troy, Mo.
Dear Folks,

   I received your letter Wed. and I was glad to hear from you. I
am O.K. and hope you are the same.

   We was called last night to help put out a fire in a guy's barn.

We didn't get there in time to put the fire out, but we did keep it away from the house.

The trucks are going to St. Louis tomorrow to see the big League game, I guess I will go.

Well, I must stop and iron a pair of pants to go to the ball game.

Goodbye and Good Luck,
Cleo T. May

Greentop, Mo., August 18, 1937
My Dear Son Cleo,

I got your letter yesterday and was glad as usual to hear from you. We are all O.K. and truly hope you are okay too. Did you have a good time at the ball game? I'll bet you did. Say, did you ever get your 70¢ back from the bus company?

Tom and Clifford are helping put up Dad's hay. Cyrus and Ted mowed it and Tom stacks it but they won't have much. They will get done today.

Do you have roasting ears to eat? We will have plenty of corn when you come home.

They got the church papered and painted, new windows put in and all fixed up for the association.

George Hendricks and Anna were supposed to come yesterday. I don't know if they did or not. Ernest Lawrence and Bud went to Iowa to find work but they both came back. Red Roy Morton was arrested last Sat. and put in jail for being drunk and reckless driving. They hung a fine on him of $25.00 and Orville pawned his Bull to George Miller to get him out.

Bill and Vina and Sol came down Sat. and Bill and Vina were remarried in Kirksville. Old Bill and Pood got so drunk that Vina had to drive home. Tom and Clifford went over there and stayed all night. Well, Cleo, I must close. There isn't any news of any interest. so write soon. Leland has him an old Model T Ford and he and Anna visits now. Paul Sorenson bought it for him and bought the license for it.

I am sending you a dime. I'd send you a dollar but I'm afraid it would get lost. I'm sending you a card, too.

Your Mother

Sunday 22, Troy, Mo. (Postcard)
Dear Folks,

I received your letter and was glad to hear from you. I was in the
hospital Sat. and Sat. night with a small boil on my arm, but it is
O.K. now. I will come home Labor Day if I am not on K.P. Well,
I must close for it is bed time. Goodbye and good luck,

Cleo

Farmington, Mo. August 28, 1937 (Postcard from Uncle Dewey)
Dear Cleo,

Recd your letter this a.m. It will be impossible as far as I know to
go home Sept. 3, but think I will go around Sept. 10, but I will
plan on staying a few days when I do go as I want to sow my
alfalfa. I know I can't go on Sept. 3 so make other arrangements. I
remain as ever your uncle,

Dewey Sevits

Sun. Aug. 29, 1937, CCC Troy, Mo.
Dear Folks,

I received your letter and was glad to hear from you. I wrote
Dewey a letter and he said he wasn't going home the 3rd of next
month. I will come home if I'm not on K.P. I can get a way home
all right for there is a boy here going to take a bunch to Kirksville.

I sure had a good time down to the ball game and zoo. I sure
seen a lot of interesting animals and snakes. I never had a better
time in my life. How is your garden stuff looking now? Does it
need rain?

Well, I must close as I don't know any more to write. I am
enclosing a clipping out of our camp paper.

Goodbye and good luck,
Cleo T. May

Again Cleo came home as planned. And again we were overjoyed
to see him. I'm sure Ma was better able to enjoy this visit than when
he came on the 4th of July. He seemed to be more grown up. I think
we all knew our big brother would never be the same. Oh, he was

glad to see us, but the uniform seemed to separate us from him. He was our returning hero.

Wed. 1937, Troy, Mo. (Postmark September 8)
Dear Folks,

I got here O.K. but I didn't make it in time for supper. I was rather glad to get back to camp. I wish I hadn't brought my suit down here; there's no decent place to keep it.

Beulah told me to write to her but I don't know her address now, so send me her address.

Goodbye and good luck,
Cleo T. May

Sun evening, Sept. 12, 1937
Dear Folks,

I am feeling O.K. and hope you are the same. It has begun to get a little chilly of nights down here. I will be glad when winter comes and maybe time will pass a little faster.

I am going to send my suit home as soon as I get the money. When you write send me a dime for stamps. I wrote Beulah a letter tonight.

Goodbye and good luck,
Cleo T. May

Greentop, Mo., Sept. 15, 1937
My Dear Son Cleo—

I got your letter yesterday and I will send you a money order this morning for 75¢ and I am sending a dime in money. This ought to last till you get your next pay.

Leland tore up his car Sat. night and now he goes horse back. He straddled a bridge banister with it. Well, there isn't any news so I will quit. It sure is cold here too. Clifford is working with Harve over to Oscar Millers helping to fill a silo. Joe May got drunk and was throwed in jail during the time that you were here.

Cleo, please don't take to drinking or smoking and for God's sake
leave cards alone. Well, please write soon and take care of yourself. I see in the paper they have sleeping sickness in St. Louis. I
hope you don't get it in the camp.

Cleo, send your suit to Mother and the mail carrier will bring it
to their house. Hope you are O.K. Write soon.

Mother

Thursday evening, Sept. 16th, 1937
Dear Mother,

I received your last two letters and money and was glad to hear
from you. I am feeling O.K. and making it fine, hope you are as
well.

You mentioned about me coming home the last of this month,
but unless you want me to do different I aim to stay this winter. I
don't believe I could get a better job this winter than I have now.

I'll not send my suit right away for I think I can sell it.

Goodbye, Write soon,
Cleo T. May

Greentop, Mo. Sept. 21, 1937
My Dear Son Cleo—

Will answer your letter I rec'd yesterday. Was glad as usual to
hear from you. We are all well and hope you are the same. It sure
has been hot here today but it hasn't rained yet and we sure do
need it. We had 2 frosts and it sure killed the tomato vines. I am
still canning things and I want to get my jars all filled. Ted and
Harve have been having an awful time gettting their silos filled
but they finally got through. Clifford is out to Dave Newcomer's
and will stay 2 weeks. I sure miss him now that the kids are going
to school. Cleve Adams came after him the day before Dave
came but Clifford wouldn't work for him.

Grandma and Grandpa have been digging their Irish potatoes
and sweet potatoes and they sure had a lot of nice ones. They
have had lots of peaches too. I want Tom to get busy and find us
a place to move just as soon as he can for we can never live in this

house this winter. I thought I'd get to go to Waterloo for Cattle Congress but I don't suppose I'll get to. Grandma wants you to write her a letter.

Did Beulah write to you? I hope the next time you come home you can stay longer.

Wednesday morning—Well, Cleo I must quit. I thought I could write more but the kids are ready to go to school. We are so busy. Write soon and send me your camp paper. I'll write again soon.

Your Mother

Cleo and friends at CCC Camp in Troy, Missouri

Two o'clock Sept 24, 1937, CCC Troy, Mo.
Dear Folks,

I received your letter and was glad to hear from you.

If you all move, send me your address in plenty of time so I will have time to change the address of the check, and don't tell unless you are sure you are going to move there.

It hasn't come a frost yet, here. It is raining here now. It has been raining since 11 o'clock. I wrote Beulah a letter but she never did answer.

I don't know when I can get a leave but I will come home as soon as I can. Well, I must close.

Goodbye
Cleo

Waterloo, Iowa, Oct. 5, 1937
Dear Cleo,

Just a few lines in answer to your letter I received several days ago. I should have written sooner but I've neglected it. We looked for Ted's up for cattle show but they didn't come. Gene and I went out one day.

Yes, Cleo I think it would be a good idea for you to stay in camp yet this winter, then next spring get a good job some where. Gene sure had bad luck while I was in Missouri. Someone robbed him of $100.00. Maby you think that didn't make me sick. But I guess I've got over it now. I thought Clifford would get to come up for the show but he didn't. There is a lot of work here now. Gene works every Sunday.

I guess you heard about Sherman's baby dying. It sure was too bad.

Well, I must close; I don't know anything to write. Will you get any more vacations? We hope to get to go home for Xmas. Well, be a good boy Cleo and write again.

With Love,
Beulah

Greentop, Mo. Oct. 12, 1937
My Dear Son Cleo—

With a very heavy heart I'll try to answer your long looked for letter I got today. I am tore up so bad I believe I'll sure go crazy. Cleo, dear child, you know I wrote you and told you that you didn't need to reinlist unless you wanted to for we can't get any help of any kind and Tom can't work on the W.P.A. since you are in camp. I saved you $29.00 and if you don't believe it I can send you the bank book. Tom went to Iowa with Pood Sunday and he is going to try to get work.

I am sending you 30 cents and it's every cent I've got and if you need money bad enough I'll draw some out and send it to you. What did you ever do with your suit? Cleo, I'll save the money like you said if I have to live on cornbread and water. I am so worried I can hardly stand it. It's too much on me for what I've already gone through with. The kids needs overshoes and underwear, but I'll save your money like you said.

I do hope you are better. Aren't you doctoring the carbuncle? Well, Cleo there isn't anything to write about and I'm so near crazy I'll close. Write just as soon as you get this so I'll know how you are. Your Grandma has been wondering why you don't write. Well, Goodbye and may God bless you and keep you from harm are the wishes from your loving

Mother

Oct. 14, 1937, CCC 3771, Troy, Mo.
Dear Folks,

I received your letter today. You know very good and well that I wouldn't take the last penny in the house if I would have been there. There wasn't any need of you sending that 30¢ if that was all you had. If it wasn't for it getting lost I would send it back. If the kids needs clothes, buy them.

But I still think you could have had more money in the bank last summer if you would have tried.

Some day you might know why I wanted the money saved.

Don't go hungry or naked on account of me, but you have went through the winter on less than that and it looks like you could do it again.

I worked on a rock wall the first of the week down by the old Hamlin House. The house was an old Negro slave plantation built in 1814. The weatherboard is solid walnut.

It has begun to get rather cold down here now. If anything ever made me want to come home it's the ducks I see flying over here lately.

Has Dad found work yet? How is everybody around there?
Well I must close.

> Goodbye and Good Luck
> Cleo T. May

Oct. 22, 1937
Dear Folks,

I received your letter and stamped envelope and was glad to
hear from you.

There was a rookie came here the other day that beat any thing
I ever saw before. The first day he was here, he got up before the
whole bunch of boys, up to the rec hall and started to sing. He
would sing one song right after another and everybody laughing
right in his face, but that didn't embarrass him at all. It sure was
funny.

There is one little boy here that isn't over 12 years old. I sure
feel sorry for him.

Now, that question you asked me. No! there isn't any such
women comes out here. When there is girls come out here some
man brings them and they are as decent as any women you know.

I would like to have the Daily but I am afraid it would cost too
much. Well I must close. Write soon.

> Cleo T. May

P.S. I haven't been to St. Louis

Greentop, Mo. Oct 25, 1937
My Dear Son Cleo,

I will just write a few lines as I'm sending you a dollar that Ted
owed you and he gave it to me so I thought you'd need it.

I hope you are fine and dandy as we are all well. I was real sick
last week, but I'm O.K. now. Forest and Florence and Mrs. Potter
came down last nite and they took me to Kirksville today.

Tom came down Sat. nite with Pood and went back yesterday
with Pood and Sol. Scott Pointer went back with them too.

When do you think you will come home for a few days?

They took Het Scott back to the hospital yesterday. I don't
know what is wrong with her.

Well, Cleo I must close. Why haven't you wrote to me? Elmer
Stephens is with Opal and they are sure having a time. Well, Cleo
please write just as soon as you get this. Tom said he was going to
write you.

Mother

Sun. eve, Oct. 31, 1937, Greentop, Mo.
My Dear Son Cleo,

I will write you a few lines tonite to tell you all that has
happened in the last week. Last Sun eve Tom started back to
Waterloo with Pood and Sol, Cap Tarr and Dorothy and their
baby, Scott Pointer and Dale Gregory and up on this side of
Oskaloosa, Iowa Pood was driving about 60 miles an hour and a
car was driving in front of him and stopped. Pood didn't have any
brakes and he didn't want to run into the car so he ran into the
bank and turned over 2 or 3 times and completely wrecked the
car and there wasn't any of them hurt seriously. Dorth and her
baby never got a scratch. Tom got hurt worse than any of them.
The patrolman took them to Oskaloosa to the hospital and they
waited there and called into Waterloo for James Fowler to come
get them. Pood drove his car to Waterloo after the wreck with all
the top, doors and glass and everything torn off of it. The engine
never stopped running. I went over to Ethel's when I heard about
it and we hired Virgil McFarland to take us there. We left
Kirksville at 9 o'clock Wednesday morning and got there at dark
that evening. We found them all able to work but Tom and I
brought him back home. I don't know when he will be able to
work hard. He is up most of the time but he is in bed quite a bit
too. Everything goes against us. He had a good job and had a
chance to make some money but he had to give it up. Dale
Gregory took his job.

The day before I left I sent a registered letter with a dollar in it.
Did you get it? Please ans. soon and tell me if you got it. The rest
of us are O.K. and hope you are the same.

Sol came home with Ethel to buy in their place over to
Connelsville for it is going to sell for taxes. When are you going to

get to come home? You don't say anything about it when you
write. Beulah and I went to the show when we were in Waterloo.

It cost me $5.00 and Ethel $5.00 to get up there and back. Tom
didn't have any money and I thought it best to go get him.

Cleo, I don't have any money to spare to send you the Daily
unless you want me to put $9.00 in the bank and then send the
paper to you. Please write soon. Tom is yelling for me to come to
bed. Hope you are O.K. This is Hallowe'en nite. If you ever start
out in a car with anyone do be careful.

> Goodbye and good luck,
> Your Mother

Sat. Oct. 30, 1937, Troy, Mo.
Dear Folks,

I received your letter and the dollar and was glad to hear from
you. I am making it alright only I have a knotted muscle on my
left leg. I have been working with a broad ax hueing white oak
poles. This is Sat. morning and we just got thru mopping the
barracks. About 45 more rookies came in and that brought the
company up to 200 men.

The most interesting speech I ever heard was made here by Mr.
Peterson, a G-Man. He told all about the Urschel kidnapping case
and how he and his men solved it. He also told the inside stuff on
many cases. He said that any case could be solved if all the details
were noted. Some men come from St. Louis once a week and talk
about different things.

You talked like you never did get my last letter. You asked me
if I wanted the Daily or not. Well, I sure would like to have it but
I'm afraid it would cost too much. It costs about $6.50 for six
months.

We started different classes this month and I am taking
carpentry and first aid, two of the best classes there is. We are
having right nice weather down here. We are supposed to have
barracks inspection this morning. Well, I guess I must close as I
can't think of any more to write.

> Goodbye and Good luck,
> Cleo T. May

Thursday nite Nov 4—Tomorrow is my 37th birthday

Greentop, Mo., Nov. 4, 1937
My Dear Son Cleo—

 I got your letter today and will write you a few lines tonite to
let you know we are all O.K. Tom isn't able to work but I think he
is getting along O.K. He is so sore all over.

 It has been trying to rain this afternoon. I expect it will turn
cold. Clifford isn't having much luck hunting. Rabbits are 10¢
each but he can't get any. Cleo, the reason I didn't write you when
I first heard Tom was hurt was because I thought I'd wait till I got
up there and see how bad he was hurt. Then I would have written
you from there if he had been hurt bad.

 When do you think you will get to come home? Looks like you
could come home for a week. I'd sure like to come down there to
see you and the camp. The kids are all O.K.

 Cleo, I think your Dad wants to write you a few lines so I'll
close and let him write. Hope you are O.K. How did your leg get?
Well, good nite and good luck to you.

                    Your Mother

(Dad's letter appears earlier in the book)

Nov. 14, 1937
Dear Folks,

 I just found out Friday that I can get Thurs., Fri., Sat. & Sun. of
Thanksgiving week. I will come home them four days provided I
get some money to come home on. If you can get some, send it to
me, but don't get any of mine out of the bank. If I get to come I
want you to have it arranged for me to go hunting. Buy some
Super-X long rifle shells for my rifle. I am alright and hope you
are all the same. Well, I must close.

                    Cleo T. May

P.S. If you send any money send it in a registered letter.

Nov. 21, 1937
Dear Folks,

I received your letter and the money order and was glad to hear
from you. If nothing unusual happens I will be home Wed. night
or Thurs. morning. It sure is cold here. We had about ½ inch of
snow. My canteen full of water froze up hanging on the foot of
my bunk.

If I miss one of my buses it sure will be cold hitchhiking. You
don't need to answer this letter because I will get home before
you could get a letter back. Leave my rifle over to Grandma's.
Well, I will close. My pencil is so short I can't hardly write.

Good bye,
Cleo

I remember this visit clearly. As it turned out, he did miss his bus
connection and had caught a ride with a trucker who was hauling a
load of posts. He had to ride in the back among the posts. When he
arrived in the middle of the night he was chilled to the bone. We
were all excited. Dad lit the kerosene lamp and stirred up the fire.
Cleo had a treat for all of us—a big four-ounce candy bar. It seemed
that we were all talking at once—asking questions, telling news and
glowing with the joy of his presence. That homecoming was the
most memorable for me.

Sunday evening Nov. 28, 1937
Dear Folks,

I got down here in time for supper tonight. The first guy I got a
ride with brought me to Monroe City about 22 miles west of
Hannibal. That didn't get me here any sooner, because I had to
wait on the bus. But it saved me a little better than a dollar. Well,
I guess I will start work on the fence tomorrow. I ran almost out
of snow down by Bowling Green and then there was almost as
much snow here as there is up there.

I aim to write Grandma a letter and then go to bed.

Good bye,
Cleo T. May

Dec. 5, 1937, CCC 3771, Troy Mo.

Dear Folks,

I will write you in answer to your letter I received the 2nd. I am alright and hope you are as well.

We haven't worked for 3 days because of cold weather, but it really hasn't been very bad. I guess I will come home Xmas if I can. If I don't get to come home then I will get to come the last five days of this month. Half of us will have to stay here and work, and the other half will go home, then when they come back us that worked can go. I think 5 days is what I will get.

I sent those 2 negatives off for 2 reprints of each. It's a little colder this morning than it has been and it looks like it might snow.

We had a show in camp last Tuesday. I don't know what I'll do for a suitcase if I come home Xmas for that one I had is tore up.

Well, I can't think of anything to write so I guess I will close. Send me a stamp the next time you write. No! I didn't type those envelopes. I had them typed.

Goodbye and Good Luck,
Cleo T. May

Dec. 8, 1937

My Dear Son Cleo—

Just a few lines in ans. to your letter I rec'd yesterday. We are all very well. Teddy has been real sick with a cold but he is better now. I do hope you are well. It's almost time for the mail carrier to come and I must hurry. I am sending you some stamps and the next time I write I'll send you the money to come home on. I'll see what I can do about a suit case. Maby I can borrow one and send it to you or I might buy one.

I'll quit now and write you more next time. I am sending 5 stamps. It's awful cold here this morning. The worst we have had.

Hope you are O.K. Please write soon and I'll send you some money next time I write. How much do you want? (This letter ends abruptly with the one below following in the same envelope.)

Dec. 9, 1937
Dear Cleo,

I am here at Sherman's and I missed the mail carrier yesterday so I am writing a few lines. I tried to buy you a cheap suit case but if I buy you a new suit case I couldn't send you much money so if I send you the money then you can do what you want to with it. I am sending you $3.00 in this letter and if Tom gets to working I will send you more than that. You let me know just as soon as you get this and I will send you a little more. Harve has a suit case. Maby I can borrow it for you. They have one at the Thrift Shop here and he wants $2.00 for it and he said if I paid some on it he would keep it for me till I could pay for it. You write me just as soon as you get this and tell me if you want me to get it and I will have him hold it for me. I am sending you some stamps so you won't have to break on your money. It sure is awful cold. Teddy has been real sick but he is better now. I heard some boys talking up in the Thrift Shop that had been in camp and one of them said he had been in a camp in Michigan and they weren't good to the boys there. I hope you don't take cold. If you do be sure and take care of your self. Well, I must quit. Clifford and I are down here and we must start home.

Please answer as soon as you get this. I will send some more if you want it. Be sure and let me know about the suit case.

Your Mother

A Christmas card postmarked Dec. 9, 1937 arrived from Cleo. The front displayed a beautiful red and green poinsettia in a gold foil insert for a pot. Inside the inscription read, "Hearty wishes for a Merry Christmas and a very happy new year."

Sun. 12, Dec 1937
Dear Folks,

I got your letter Sat and the three dollar money order. I am alright except a slight cold in my head. As to the suitcase, you don't need to buy one up there because the way you wrote they must be pretty high. I can buy a good suitcase here for $1.00 just like the one I brought home the other time.

The $3.00 you sent will bring me home but how am I to get back? I would rather be sure of the bus fare before I start. If you can send me three more dollars I will be sure and come and as far as the suitcase is concerned I can do without it. I sent some Xmas cards. Did you get yours?

I will probably leave here the night of the 20th although I am not sure. Is there any snow up there? There isn't any here. We have missed lots of work in the last week.

I ordered myself a new locker. I will start paying for it next payday. They cost $3.75 and we pay a dollar the first 2 months and 75¢ the last month.

If you can send the money send it right away. If you can't let me know as soon as possible. I must close.

                              Goodbye and Good luck,
                              Cleo T. May

Cleo came home for one of the most bleak Christmases our family had ever known. Our food supply was practically non-existent. The only money coming in was the $25.00 a month from Cleo's earnings. Dad was still unable to work, even if work had been available. It must have been discouraging for Cleo, too.

Greentop, Mo. Dec. 30, 1937
My Dear Son Cleo,

Will answer your letter I rec'd yesterday and it's got me worried to death about you. I knew that sooner or later you would take a terrible cold going bareheaded and with light weight underwear on. Cleo, please dress different for your own sake and mine, too. I do hope you are better and what ever you do don't try to work till you are absolutely able for after having a heavy cold it would be too bad if you took a relapse.

The weather is awful here. It's been raining all this week. I have the blues so bad I don't know what to do. This place is a lob-lolly of mud. I wish I had never moved here. Clifford and Tom worked yesterday and the day before over to Charley Mikels.

What time did you get down there Sunday? Cleo did you get

the letter I sent you before you came home with the $2.00 in it?
I'm sure you did but I just want to know for sure for if you didn't
I can make the post office give it back to me. Monday we got a
box of candy and cookies from Opal so I am sending you a box
this morning. I hope you are feeling lots better when you get this.
Now Cleo you write me right back and let me know how you are
for you know I'm worried about you. If you get bad sick and
want me to come or want us for anything you call to Fred Evans
and they can come and tell us. They are on the Kirksville line and
they live right here by us and we could get the word right away.

Well, Cleo I will close now. Do take care of your self and write
me at once and tell me if you get your package. So good bye and
wishing you a speedy recovery.

Your Mother

Jan 2, 1938
Dear Folks,

I received your letter Friday and the package today. I got out
of the hospital Sat. morning and I am feeling fine now. I hope you
are all well. You don't need to worry at all about me now because
I am alright. We have been quarrnteened (quarantined) for about
a week because of Scarlet Fever.

You asked me what time I got down here. I guess it was about
5:30 when I got here to camp. Any way I missed my supper.

Yes, of course, I got the $2.00 money order. I sure did enjoy the
box and the candy.

I want you to put $4.00 in the bank for me this month. That will
be $40.00. I wish you would try to have $50.00 in the bank for me
by the time I get home. I don't think $50.00 would be too much
for a year's work, do you?

We had a good dinner New Year's. I want you to get me Beulah's address. I wrote her a letter but she never did answer.

Some time during the month I wish you would send me a dollar
to buy some hair tonic. Lucky Tiger, which I believe is the best
there is costs a dollar. This old hair oil I get here at the canteen is
ruining my hair and I can't buy any over to town because I never
have any cash. Well, I guess I must close.

Goodbye and Good Luck,
Cleo T. May

Novinger, Mo., Jan 4, 1938
Dear Cleo,

I will write you a few lines to let you know we are alive yet. But I have a bad cold. But I guess it will leave. The weather is fine— Sunshine and warm and dry. Dee Van's buried another one of their children today. It sure is bad. John Glaspie is in a hospital with the pneumonia and very bad. Beck is running his car day and night. Run out of gas and had to leave it on the road side. It takes all his money for gas. Clifford is staying at Harve's now doing his chores. He is hauling coal every day now. Well, I'll close now. Write soon.

Good bye
W.E. Sevits (Grandpa)

In the same envelope is a letter from Grandma. The handwriting is very difficult to decipher.

Dear Cleo,

How are you? Truly glad you are well again. We were worried about you. I wish you were here now and see how nice it is. No mud, no snow or ice. Just like spring. Hope it is nice where you are.

Dee Van's little boy was buried today. It died from Scarlet Fever. That is two out of their family.

How is the weather where you are? Clifford is doing Harvey's chores now. Him and Ted have so much coal to haul he needs someone to do their chores.

I will bake some cookies Thursday. Then we will go to the store Friday. Sat. I will have some change to send you some. I will send some to one of my cousins in the Dalles, Oregon and I must send Monte Peterson a little box too. I am so glad the ice and snow is gone. Hope we don't have any more snow.

We had your Mother, James and Roena, all of Harveys, Ted and Lola, Fred and Het Scott, Wendell, Basil and Freddy and we all had a nice time. Had a good and nice dinner, too. The boys wished for you.

My love and all best wishes to you
From your Loving Grandmother
Write soon. Bye bye.

Jan 6, 1938, CCC 3771, Troy, Mo.

Dear Folks,

I will write you a few lines to let you know I am alright and hope you are the same. I received your letter today. I got a letter from Grandma and one from Beulah.

I am going to send the camp paper. I don't know whether you'll get it or not.

I have been working pretty hard the last week. We have been digging a basement for a pump house and ran into solid rock.

I sure would appreciate the Daily. Beulah said she was going to send me a present for my birthday. I hope you can keep the kids in school.

Well, I must close as it is getting late.

Good bye and good luck
Cleo T. May

Jan 10, 1938

Greentop, Mo.

Dear Son Cleo,

Will write you a few lines in answer to your letter rec'd Sat. Was glad as usual to hear from you. Glad that you are feeling O.K. We had nice weather all last week but it's cloudy this morning. Looks like it might snow.

Mary Ann and her man came to Yadon's Sat. nite and they had a charivari and me and the kids went. There was a big crowd there. I believe he is a good boy. They have a job on a farm in Macon County, $27.00 per month and cows to milk.

I sent you the paper Sat. so you tell me when you write if you are getting it. I put the $4.00 in the bank and the money that was there had drawn 12 cents interest, so now there is $40.12 in the bank.

I am sending you $1.00 today and if I were you I sure wouldn't fool with that hair oil.

Mother sent you some cookies, did you get them? Clifford is still over to Harve's. Ted and Harve are real busy hauling coal and corn. Dee VanLaninghams burnt up everything they couldn't wash and they (the people at the church) took up a collection and bought new.

I bought groceries and things for the kids' buckets to last 2 weeks and paid Harve for moving us out here and gave Mother $3.00. So you see there is always a place for every cent of it.

Please write soon and tell me if you get everything or not. We never got the camp paper yet. Well, good bye and good luck and God bless you.

Your Mother

P.S. There sure is lots of Scarlet Fever up here. I'm awful afraid the kids will get it.

Sat. morning, Jan 15, 1938, Greentop, Mo.

My Dear Son Cleo,

I will write you a few lines in answer to your letter I rec'd yesterday. Was glad to hear from you and glad you are O.K. I got the camp paper Monday and was real glad to get it.

Clifford is still over to Harve's. He hasn't been home since he went over there.

No, we haven't got any snow up here. It tried to snow one day this week but just a little. It's real nice today. I sure hope we don't have any bad weather. I don't know much to write. I haven't been any where and haven't seen any one so I don't know any thing new. We are all O.K. and hope you are the same. I forgot to tell you in my other letter that Joe was over to Yadons the nite of the charivari and was dog drunk and had a revolver strapped on a belt. Him and Pood are going to Waterloo next week they say.

Harve May's are quarantined with Scarlet Fever. Dorothy had it and I don't know if the baby took it or not. Has there been any more cases of it in camp?

The kids went to school all last week but half of the school kids are not coming on account of Scarlet Fever.

Well, Cleo I will close. Nothing more to write about. Hope you are O.K. and write soon.

Your Mother

Greentop, Mo. Jan 21, 1938

My Dear Son Cleo,

Will ans. your letter I got yesterday. Was glad to hear from you and that you are O.K. Boy the weather is awful here. Gloomy and muddy. Cleo I am sending you 4 stamps. Maby I can send you a little spending money before pay day. If I can get hold of any. Have you decided when you will come home again? Clifford hasn't come home from Harves. I may go over home tonite if it isn't bad. I get homesick to go over there. I like this place better than I did. I have been going to Sublette to church and I have got acquainted with people around here. The kids and I went to Sublette Wed. nite to hear a missionary from Roumania. He has been in 19 countries and also the Holy Land and speaks 12 languages. He was to go to Union last nite but it's so muddy I don't think he got there. Ted never did start his barn. I guess he and Harve are real busy hauling.

Beulah said Gene would be out of work in about 2 weeks and then they were coming down here.

Tom got something in his eye last week and he went to the doctor and he put something in it to enlarge the sight. It never has gone back to normal yet. He looks comical but his eye still hurts.

Have you ever been released from the quarantine? The kids are O.K. and in school. Write soon and let me know how you are.

> Goodbye and lots of luck
> Your Mother

Postmark Jan 22, Waterloo, Iowa
(A post card with a photograph of the Wrigley Building in Chicago and the notation, "The landlady gave me this card," from Beulah)

Dear Cleo,

Just a few lines to tell you I am sending you a watch next week. I will send it Monday so you can look for it. I hope you like it. I wish I could have got you a better one. Write me as soon as you get it. We are all fine. Hope you are well.

> Love, Beulah

(A birthday card from Mother and all dated Jan 26, 1938)

A thousand good wishes for your Birthday

> Mother and All to Cleo
> XXXXXXXX

Greentop, Mo. Feb 25, 1938

My Dear Son Cleo—

I should have wrote you yesterday but I was over to Mother's and the mail carrier had gone before I got home.

Dauber is holding a meeting at Union and Brother Davis went there Wednesday nite just for one nite. So I went over and stayed all night to go to church. We are all pretty well. Teddy is O.K. His leg is healing fine. I hope you are O.K. The sun is shining so nice this morning the first for a long time.

We wrote Sol's a letter to see if we could get their house a while but Ethel wrote back and said Sol might get layed off any time and if he did they would have to come back. Their address is: P.S. May, 206 Duryea St., Waterloo, Iowa.

Cleo I wrote Harve May a letter and asked him if he would sell his gun and if he will would it be O.K. to buy it for you. I promised you a gun and I'll get it. We haven't found a place to move yet. I don't know where we will go.

Beulah and Gene came by here from Kirksville yesterday and went over to Mothers. Harve and Ted never came home last weekend at all. The scarlet fever is raging here again. They shut down Mulberry school. The measles are raging too. I'm afraid that Shirley got exposed to whooping cough up to Sublette.

If I can get that gun from Harve would it suit you or not? You be sure and tell me when you write so I'll know what I'm doing.

Tom says that 10 gauge shot gun down to the second hand store would be a good one, but you tell me just what I must do and I'll do it. So write soon and hope you are O.K. You send me the camp paper when you get it.

Mother

Novinger, Mo., Feb 22, 1938

Dear Cleo,

I will write you a few lines to let you know we are all O.K. and hope this finds you the same. We had a snow last night. But it is nearly gone. Your Pa and Ma was here today. Just went home. They may get to stay where they are at. That man said he would not have to move there. Clifford is still at Harve's. Well, I will close. Write soon.

Good bye, W.E. Sevits

Waterloo, Iowa, 206 Duryea St., March 1, 1938
Dear Cousin Cleo,

I will answer your letter we just received. Was glad to hear
from you. I am not feeling very good. I fell out of a tree about 20
feet high and broke my left arm and broke some bones in my
right hand. So you see I am not in very good shape for duck hunting right now. But hope to be a little better later on. I expect to
have my arm in a cast for 6 weeks or longer. I sure had bad luck.

That was sure a good picture of you and me hunting ducks. I
will try my best to be down there when you are if my arm gets
along O.K. Well, Cleo work here don't look very good right now.
They are laying off down there at John Deere's. Lissie's man got
layed off and Dad might get it any time. But if anything opens up
we will let you know.

I am going to start storing away the shells for duck hunting.
Pood has not worked a day since he came back this last time. I
missed you the last time you was home. I didn't know what day
you would be there. I had a birthday February 13. Dad gave me 5
dollars.

You know when I fell Cleo, I liked to broke my neck too. I fell
right on my head and neck and I hurt my nose, too. I fell Feb
28th. I sure wish my arm would hurry and get well. It is sure
awful to be layed up.

Well, Cleo, I will close so answer real soon for I am lonesome.
Good Bye.

                                    From Joe May to Cleo

Greentop, Mo. R2, Mar. 3, 1938
My Dear Son Cleo,

I will answer your letter we got yesterday. It found us just
pretty good. James has been having sore throat but it isn't bad.
Hope you are O.K. It is rainy this morning. It has been real nice
weather up until this morning. Yes, Cleo I will order your gun just
as soon as the check comes regardless of what anyone says. The
check will come next Tuesday or Wed. Clifford told me that he
and Ted saw you on the bus that day and I forgot to say anything
to you about it.

The man that was going to move here moved back to Albia,

Iowa and Tom wrote Sloan a letter to see if we could live here till the first of April, but we haven't heard from him yet.

Tuesday of this week a bunch of men came here to the house and wanted a drink and Vic (Dad's brother) was in the bunch and he didn't know we lived here. He told me that we might rent the George Billington house at Shibley's Point. Tom is going to see about it Saturday. Well, Cleo there isn't much to write about so I will close. Don't worry about the gun for I will order it just as soon as I get the check.

Tom is working at Barnes and Clifford never has been home since he went over to Ted and Harves. Well, I will quit and you write soon as you get this. Hope you are O.K. I saw lots of ducks going over yesterday. Oh yes, a week ago Sunday a tramp came up to the door and wanted to come in and warm and I let him in and then he wanted something to eat. I gave him what I had and then on Tuesday nite about midnite someone knocked on the door and wanted in but we didn't let him in.

Hershel and Fern are moving back right away. Well, I will close. Ans. soon and don't worry about anything.

Wendell and Basil were converted in the meeting at Union.

Your Mother

March 10, 1938
Dear Cleo,

How are you? I am all right. It rained here night before last and it is still cloudy. Ma said she would get the gun you wanted. I hope this month goes fast. I saw a bunch of geese yesterday.

Your brother, James

18th day of the 3rd month of the 38th year of the 20th century
CCC 3771, Troy, Missouri
Dear Folks,

What is wrong with you? Did you run out of stamps? I figured you had for you sent me a post card in answer to my letter. We had a chicken supper tonight and every one that was going out had to make a little stub speech.

There's a transfer for 22 men to Calif. next month and if it wasn't for the fires out there I would sign up again and go out there.

I took two rolls of film. I have been laying rock this week. How is the weather up there? It is just like spring down here. We will have to start cutting the grass before long.

Well, I must close as I am running out of anything to say.

Good bye,

Cleo T. May

Greentop, Mo., Mar. 22, 1938

My Dear Son Cleo—

I will answer your letter I rec'd yesterday. Was glad as usual to hear from you and glad you are O.K. We are all well.

We are certainly having spring weather. It's so hot you can hardly stay in the house to cook and eat.

Cleo, you had me guessed right when you thought I didn't have any stamps for I sure didn't, but I thought you would understand. You know how it is with me. There wasn't much left out of the check this month after I got the gun and gave Mother $5.00 and bought a few groceries and a couple pair of shoes.

Cleo, I don't want you to sign up to go to California. I didn't want you to sign up the last time and you did any way. It certainly would cost something to come home if you were in California and you surely wouldn't want to stay away 6 months and you know how dangerous it is out there about floods and forest fires. I don't have much say about my family any more it seems but if you go you sure will go against my will.

Beulah and Gene bought the Ben Halley place. Cleo, I put your gun away and it isn't put together. It's in the box it came in. It's a Stevens gun but says Long Tom on the box, but it is a Stevens.

Lois Scott is lots better now. They didn't think for a while that she would live.

Well, I must close and get to work. Please write soon for I am always anxious to hear from you. John Deere is still laying off men so I suppose Sol's will be down here on relief before long. Hope you are fine and write soon. The kids are in school and Clifford is still at Harve's.

Your Mother

Ma's emphatic opposition to Cleo's plans to re-enlist must have been convincing because he chose an honorable discharge instead. We were living near the old mine in the Hungry Hollow school district when he got out, but Dad had been looking for a place to move closer to the WPA project at the limestone quarry. Cleo's first order of business was to help us move to Sublette, a tiny rural community with a general store, two filling stations and a church.

As soon as the move was completed, Cleo revealed his reason for wanting $50 in savings. He had spent most of his free time during the two six-month hitches planning for the day when he could come home and buy his own car. The appointed day had come. He drew out his money and headed to Kirksville to a used car dealer to pick out the "right" car. The first automobile to grace our family was the 1926 Chevrolet touring sedan that Cleo selected. The dealer, after learning the amount of money Cleo possessed, tailored the price to equal that amount. He sold the tire tool, jack and crank as optional equipment. But no matter, at long last Cleo would have his own transportation. Somehow those 12 months of hard work now all seemed worthwhile. The 12-year-old vehicle had surely seen better days, but Cleo kept it running just fine with his constant tinkering.

And better still, he took us everywhere—to church, to Grandma's, into Kirksville to the picture show or just about any place we wanted to go. His own car gave him more latitude, too. Cleo's circle of friends widened, including a girl friend in Queen City.

Now all he needed was a job.

Chapter Thirteen

Living on High in the City

It was inevitable that we would move to the city. In addition to the fact that the WPA had a large street building project in Kirksville, there were more opportunities for work for the older boys.

With fear and trembling we arrived at 815 North High Street on May 1, 1940. High Street, one of the beautiful residential streets of Kirksville, was bounded at the south end by the campus of the Northeast Missouri State Teachers College. Tastefully interspersed among the stately houses along the tree-lined brick-paved street, churches and the Masonic Temple graced the neighborhoods. This beauty ended abruptly with the cinder-paved 800 block at the north end, bounded by the CB&Q Railroad tracks. The house itself, another square, pyramid-roofed $8-a-month former mine-house, afforded no more comforts than the country houses. The fact that we were forced to share the well and an inadequate outdoor toilet with next-door neighbors whose house was owned by the same landlord created problems we had heretofore not faced. But we adapted.

Because our country school year had finished about the middle of April and the city schools didn't end until the last of May, we school-age kids found ourselves with time on our hands. We took advantage of the situation by knocking on doors looking for odd jobs. We also began to scout out sources of supply for fuel. The Missouri Power and Light Company burned coal taken from cars along the railroad. Because it was a short distance down the tracks from our house, Milton, Jimmy, Robert and I took turns going in twos to pick up the coal which spilled over the sides of the conveyor. We carried it home in buckets or gunny sacks and later somehow acquired a wheelbarrow.

We made friends with the railroad section crew whose foreman unloaded used railroad ties strategically by our house. One day while Dad was at work and Ma had taken a house cleaning job for an elderly couple in the country, the section hands dumped a fine load of ties right next to Dad's chopping block. Our next-door neighbor, a simple minded child living in a huge man's body, seized the opportunity, in the absence of our folks, to transfer the readily available fuel supply to his own backyard. I, who had been left in charge of the house and my younger brothers and sister, was shocked to see big Ed blatantly carrying away Dad's ties. I had been tidying up our coal pile and had a shovel in my hands when I confronted him.

"Ed," I called to him, "do you know those are Dad's ties?"

"Who says?" retorted Ed.

"The section foreman, that's who," I replied firmly.

"Well now, the section foreman ain't here and neither is Tom and you sure can't stop me," he stated emphatically as he continued carrying the ties away.

"Now, you listen here, Ed. You know those ties are Dad's and you'll be sorry. Just wait and see," I said with a firm gesture with my shovel.

"You'll be the one to be sorry," Ed countered.

Within minutes a car drove up and a rap came at the door. We hid under the bed, but when the knocking persisted, I fearfully opened the door. There stood a man who appeared to be ten feet tall. It was the county juvenile officer. He warned us that he could take us to jail for threatening our neighbor and that we had not heard the last of it.

Pale and terror-stricken when Ma returned, we told our story. Appalled, she sent one of us across the street to the filling station to call a taxi so she could go to the home of the officer to get to the bottom of the matter. When Ma explained all the facts to him, the juvenile officer apologized. But we would not soon forget our brush with the law even though the officer ordered Ed to return the ties he had taken from our yard. When Dad got home he told Ed he could keep what he had and that in the future we would share whatever the section hands unloaded.

In addition to the railroad ties and stoker coal, we utilized yet another source of fuel for heat and cooking. The feed mill bought corn from farmers, shelled and ground it into feed for livestock. Corn cobs became a by-product of the shelling process. We could have all we could carry at five cents per gunny sack full. I shall always remember the embarrassment I experienced when one day as I walked bent over, carrying a gunny sack of cobs on my back, I met head on with one of my new school friends, the boy who played the bugle for the flag raising ceremonies each morning. He was friendly, though, and paid no particular attention to my embarrassing burden.

The one-room, eight-grade country schools had given us a peek at the outside world through a tiny window, but the city schools opened wide the door. Most city youngsters entered junior high in the seventh grade and country students came in on buses in the ninth grade. It was slightly awkward for me to enter junior high in the eighth grade. My biggest adjustment problem came from the fact that I was two years younger than my peers. At this developing age of a young adolescent, two years can be crucial. Because of my diminutive size and lack of physical development, I became the subject of unmerciful teasing. I was too short to be chosen for volleyball until all the taller girls had been picked. I learned personal hygiene quickly in the after-gym showers and soon learned to set my hair in pin curls. But what I lacked in physical development, I made up for in moxie. When Mr. Goetze, the music teacher, asked for a volunteer to lead the singing, I stood up. I had never heard Tchaikovsky's "None But The Lonely Heart," but from that day forward it became one of my special favorites. When Miss Lowe, the speech and drama teacher needed actors, I was always available. And when our home room was asked to supply a hula dancer for the school carnival, I donned a shredded paper skirt and a home made lei and danced the hula.

Miss Swartz' eighth grade home room at the west door of Ophelia Parrish Junior High, showing off track and field ribbons

Because learning came easily for me, I was invited to evening homework sessions with the girls in my class who lived on the better part of High Street. They gave me their outgrown clothes and helped me with hair styles in exchange for answers to tough math problems. The relationship was mutually beneficial and I made some lasting friendships.

Mr. Thoburn Hawk, perhaps the most memorable of all the junior high teachers, engaged in a unique practice in his social science classes. While most of the teachers saw candy and gum as disciplinary problems in their classes, Mr. Hawk's solution was simple: If you want to chew gum or eat candy, bring enough for everyone. It became a real occasion for sharing for me to be able to save up enough money to bring a piece of candy or gum for all my classmates. But teaching was his real forte. Resting comfortably on his crutches—his legs were paralyzed—he patiently explained the constitution and the democratic process. We held mock elections and discussed candidates, but we never discovered his political leanings.

I learned to cook a variety of foods and to sew in the household arts class. Pride nearly overcame me when I was invited to model the dress I had made in a fashion show for school assembly.

My favorite English teacher, Miss Swartz, was also my home room adviser. She showed a special personal concern for my brother Jimmy and me. She arranged, very discreetly, for us to attend the annual Thanksgiving dinner given for underprivileged children by the Shriners at the Masonic Temple. She sent us to the NYA sewing room for dresses, shirts and trousers. And for the last day of school, she took the whole class to the Ownbey Lake for a picnic. There, at the dance pavilion to the beat of the juke box playing "Jersey Bounce" and "Elmer's Tune," I learned to dance.

When summer came we walked east of town on the railroad tracks and found new berry patches. Then, when we got back to town around noon, we knocked on doors until we sold what we had picked. We turned the money over to Ma automatically.

When the restrictions were lifted that permitted only one family member to participate in work programs at a time, Cliff and Milton joined the CCC. Cliff finished his six-month hitch, but Milton, a confirmed free spirit, was unable to cope with the regimented life. Ma persuaded the authorities to release him, with the promise that he would take a farm job for the same period. She found a farm family who would give him board and room and provide him with some new clothes as payment for working six months.

Cliff and Cleo got jobs unloading gravel from rail cars to dump trucks for the NYA and later were hired by the state highway department. They bought their lunch provisions daily at the little grocery store near us. A slice of baloney, a five-cent loaf of bread and a little cake brought the total to about 15 cents. They earned about $1.50 per day. But work in the winter months was much more difficult to find.

Just as world events had contributed to the beginning of the Great Depression, global happenings shaped the end of it. Hitler had begun his relentless march for power and after his invasion of Poland on September 1, 1939, Britain and France declared war on Germany. Because they had been our long time allies, President Roosevelt rallied Americans to their cause and proposed that the United States should become "the great arsenal of democracy," by supplying war materials through sale, loan or lease.

When our allies had used up all available funds near the end of 1940, the President called for and got the Lend-Lease Act on March 11, 1941.

In our role as the "great arsenal of democracy," factories geared up for higher production. Farmers who previously had no market for their grain and livestock were encouraged by the government to cultivate every available inch of their soil for maximum food production. In addition to being democracy's arsenal, the United States became the bread basket for the free world.

The advent of the Selective Training and Service Act on September 16, 1940 brought the mobilization of thousands of unemployed young men. So, it was World War II that actually brought the end to the Great Depression. Economically, we would never be the same, but the war brought a more heart-breaking kind of deprivation. Separation from family, in many cases permanently, of sons, brothers, husbands and fathers hurt more than the lack of food or comfort.

In March, 1941 Cleo persuaded Dad and Ma to let him join the U.S. Coast Guard. Talk of war and conscription were viable arguments for enlisting in the service of one's choice rather than being drafted into the army. Reluctantly, Ma and Dad agreed and again their first-born son left home, this time to New Orleans, Louisiana, for military training. He was able to send Ma an allowance that was matched by government funds. Ma, along with other mothers of sons in the Navy and Coast Guard created the charter for a Navy Mothers Chapter.

Cleo on his first visit home looking happy and handsome in his new sailor uniform

Our pride is showing even though Cliff has fat cheeks from the mumps

The first time he came home in the summer of 1941 we were so proud of him. He was handsome in his sailor suit and so sophisticated. Ma wanted to do something special to honor his homecoming and planned to bake his favorite coconut cream pie. Robert and I went out real early to pick blackberries to sell for enough money to buy the needed ingredients. We were home by noon with the proceeds from about four gallons of berries at 30 cents a gallon. While Ma built up a hot fire in the cookstove, she sent Robert to the store for milk, cream, eggs and coconut. She began to make the pie dough for the crust. While the crusts baked she cooked the cream filling and beat the egg whites stiffly for meringue. Now all that remained was to toast the meringue sprinkled with shredded coconut in the hot oven. When Ma pulled out the rusty oven rack to rotate the pies for even browning, the one at the back slid off into the ash-covered bottom of the oven. what a disaster! Ma had planned a celebration for the whole family, but now there would only be enough pie for a few. She asked for volunteers to abstain. If she and we older ones didn't take any, there would be enough for Cleo, Dad and the little ones, with seconds for Cleo if he wanted. We were happy to sacrifice. After all, we could have pie another time. Cleo would only be home a short time.

In Kirksville we soon became aware of recreation and entertainment which had previously been unavailable to us. Three movie theaters were within walking distance. And the admission was as low as ten cents for matinees with special Saturday morning shows for kids that required six bread wrappers or Pepsi Cola bottle caps. We could always pick up the bottle caps at the filling station and the families in the neighborhood shared their bread wrappers with us.

Within a few blocks of our home a small city park provided a shallow swimming and wading pool for children under 12. Robert, Shirley, Teddy and I spent most of our summer afternoons splashing in the cool water.

Summer passed quickly. Fall brought the beginning of school again. I *loved* ninth grade. I was being accepted as a peer even with the difference in age. I delighted in algebra and Latin, and the school dances.

Young men in military uniforms were beginning to be a common sight on the streets around the courthouse square. Cleo was due to come home on leave the first week in December. On Sunday, December 7, when we were all gathered together for a family celebration, the news came over the radio that Pearl Harbor had been attacked by the Japanese. Along with that announcement came the order for all military personnel to return to their bases at once. We had no real idea where or what Pearl Harbor was. We did know that we were now at war and Cleo was our tangible link to that terrible consequence.

The next day, listening intently as we gathered around the radio in a general assembly at school, we heard President Roosevelt ask for a declaration of war calling the Japanese action "a day that will live in infamy."

Ultimately all my six brothers gave active military service to their country. Cleo, Cliff, Milton and Jimmy fulfilled their duties during World War II. Both Robert and Teddy served in the U.S. Army during the Korean conflict.

Cleo spent most of his service time aboard the U.S. Coast Guard Ship *Monomoy* in the North Atlantic. Milton and Cliff, assigned to

Date explains the somber expression—
December 7, 1941

two separate regiments of the Third Armored Division, spearheaded through Europe until Milton was killed in Belgium in January, 1945. Cliff was among the men of the liberating force on VE Day, May 8, 1945. Ironically, Cliff died in an auto crash in 1953. Jimmy, who at 17 was the youngest at the time of his induction, was stationed for nearly 30 months on Eniwetok Atoll in the Pacific Ocean on active duty with the Navy. He had convinced Dad to let him join early so he could be on a ship.

The war's demand for higher production provided Dad with full time farm work for the duration and for several years to come. The boys sent Ma an allowance from their monthly pay. My younger brothers, sister and I reaped the benefits of a higher standard of living. For the first time since their marriage, Dad and Ma lived in a modern house within walking distance of shopping, schools and churches.

The "Hungry Years" had ended. But World War II brought a different kind of suffering. The kind of hunger that comes from longing for the return of loved ones and for an end to killing totally overshadowed the suffering of the Great Depression. But that is another time and another story.

BOLDBLUE JAY PUBLICATIONS

For additional copies of *The Hungry Years*

Use handy order blank below. Excellent gifts for friends, relatives or co-workers. A fine teaching aid for units on the Great Depression.

Single copy	$5.95
Postage/handling	1.00
TOTAL	$6.95

Minnesota residents add 30 cents sales tax

QUANTITY DISCOUNTS
Dealer inquiries invited. Fund-raisers, clubs, groups too.

MAKE CHECKS PAYABLE TO:
Bold Blue Jay Publications

Call or write for information.

Return order blank to:
Bold Blue Jay Publications
229 Moonlite Drive
Circle Pines, MN 55014
Telephone 612-784-7522

Name _____

Address _____

City _____State _____Zip _____

Phone _____

Please send me _____ copy(s) of *The Hungry Years*

Enclosed is: Book price $ _____ Handling $ _____

Sales tax (MN only) _____ Total enclosed $ _____

Name _____

Address _____

City _____State _____Zip _____

Phone _____

Please send me _____ copy(s) of *The Hungry Years*

Enclosed is: Book price $ _____ Handling $ _____

Sales tax (MN only) _____ Total enclosed $ _____